The College Student's Guide to

Research Papers

101 Ways to Make Your Work Stand Out

By Jessica Piper

THE COLLEGE STUDENT'S GUIDE TO RESEARCH PAPERS: 101 WAYS TO MAKE YOUR WORK STAND OUT

1405 SW 6th Avenue • Ocala, Florida 34471 • Phone 800-814-1132 • Fax 352-622-1875
Website: www.atlantic-pub.com • Email: sales@atlantic-pub.com
SAN Number: 268-1250

Library of Congress Cataloging-in-Publication Data

Names: Piper, Jessica E., 1994- author.
Title: The college student's guide to research papers : 101 ways to make your work stand out / Jessica Piper.
Description: Ocala, Florida : Atlantic Publishing Group, Inc, 2017. | Includes bibliographical references and index.
Identifiers: LCCN 2017035032 (print) | LCCN 2017045007 (ebook) | ISBN 9781620231869 (ebook) | ISBN 9781620231852 (alk. paper) | ISBN 1620231859 (alk. paper)
Subjects: LCSH: Report writing—Handbooks, manuals, etc. | Research—Handbooks, manuals, etc.
Classification: LCC LB2369 (ebook) | LCC LB2369 .P498 2017 (print) | DDC 808.06/6378—dc23
LC record available at https://lccn.loc.gov/2017035032

Printed in the United States

PROJECT MANAGER: Danielle Lieneman
ASSISTANT EDITOR: Kristen Joseph
INTERIOR LAYOUT AND JACKET DESIGN: Nicole Sturk

Reduce. Reuse.
RECYCLE.

A decade ago, Atlantic Publishing signed the Green Press Initiative. These guidelines promote environmentally friendly practices, such as using recycled stock and vegetable-based inks, avoiding waste, choosing energy-efficient resources, and promoting a no-pulping policy. We now use 100-percent recycled stock on all our books. The results: in one year, switching to post-consumer recycled stock saved 24 mature trees, 5,000 gallons of water, the equivalent of the total energy used for one home in a year, and the equivalent of the greenhouse gases from one car driven for a year.

Over the years, we have adopted a number of dogs from rescues and shelters. First there was Bear and after he passed, Ginger and Scout. Now, we have Kira, another rescue. They have brought immense joy and love not just into our lives, but into the lives of all who met them.

We want you to know a portion of the profits of this book will be donated in Bear, Ginger and Scout's memory to local animal shelters, parks, conservation organizations, and other individuals and nonprofit organizations in need of assistance.

– Douglas & Sherri Brown,
President & Vice-President of Atlantic Publishing

Table of Contents

Foreword 9

Introduction 13

Chapter 1: What Is A Research Paper? 15

Research Papers In College 16

Types of research papers 17

The importance of timing 17

Questions To Ask Before You Begin 19

Chapter 2: Planning Your Paper 21

Choosing Your Topic 22

Narrowing a broad topic 23

The Thesis Statement 23

Thesis statement formulas 24

Example thesis statements 25

Ways To Organize 28

Brainstorming and prewriting 30

Chapter 3: Beginning Your Research 35

What Counts As A Source? 36

Conducting an experiment 36

Primary, Secondary, and Tertiary Sources 37

The Purpose Of Sources 39

Evaluating sources...40

Where To Look...43

Books are great 44

Discovering databases 45

Internet research.. 46

Chapter 4: Constructing Your Argument 51

Your Thesis And Beyond..51

Using evidence.. 52

Organizing your research 56

Considering Alternative Perspectives.......................................58

When you encounter conflicting evidence............................... 59

Chapter 5: Avoiding Plagiarism 63

What Is Plagiarism? 64

Obvious plagiarism 65

Paraphrasing and summarizing 65

Quoting and misquoting 68

Consequences of plagiarism 70

Citation Styles..70

MLA style... 71

APA style... 73

Turabian/Chicago style 74

The bibliography 76

Check yourself.. 77

Chapter 6: The Body Of Your Paper 79

Thinking About Writing.. 80

Supporting Your Thesis 82

Backing up your claims 82

Structuring Your Paper 84

How to organize your ideas.................................... 84

(Maybe) not just words 87

Research Paper Style 88

Types of sentences 89

Incorporating quotes 97

Keep in mind 100

Chapter 7: Introductions And Conclusions....................................103

Your Intro 103

Your hook.. 105

Transitioning to your thesis.................................... 112

Your Conclusion.. 114

Restating your thesis.. 115

Going over key points 116

Making it memorable 117

Chapter 8: Editing And Revising 121

The Difference Between Editing And Revising................124

Questions to ask while you are revising................ 124

Basic Editing Tips 126

Beyond spell-check.. 126

Chapter 9: Common Writing Mistakes 131

   Things To Watch Out For 132

      Homophones *132*

      The punctuation situation *135*

      Other writing notes *143*

   The Power of Less 144

      The word count issue *145*

      Writing concisely *146*

Chapter 10: The Finishing Touches 149

   The Title 150

   Formatting Your Paper 151

      Why formatting matters *152*

      How to format *152*

   Afterwards 154

      Don't stop learning *155*

Conclusion 157

Author's Note 161

Glossary 165

Bibliography 171

Index 173

Foreword

Effective communication is everything.

Without it, our world would be one of nonsense, vociferous argument, and chaos. There's a reason better communicators are more successful. Hospitals, schools, gyms, laboratories, and construction sites all require excellent communicators — albeit in markedly different ways.

As I am fond of telling my students, becoming an effective communicator matters in every discipline. Knowing how to write well is at the heart of that most essential of skills. The scientists, novelists, and philosophers that hang on the tips of our tongues are there not just for their accomplishments, but also for their ability to communicate their ideas to the world. They write books, publish papers, give speeches, and engage in public discourse. Most of them learned how to do these things by attending a college somewhere. They learned how to conduct and analyze research, avoid comma splices, synthesize sources, master paragraph structure, avoid fallacies, and so on.

Without effective oral and written communication, our world would be a far less enjoyable place — and definitely a more chaotic one. After all, some of the most important moments in United States history occurred in the written form. Many of those documents, such as *The Declaration of Independence*, changed the face of this country forever. Others made seemingly compelling arguments in favor of retrospectively immoral acts, such as the internment of Japanese Americans during the Second World War. Becoming a better writer overall means becoming a better thinker. As you begin to understand how to construct arguments, conduct in-depth research, and revise your writing, you'll also begin to see how the written word can be a force for change, both good and bad.

There are, of course, many different kinds of communication. This book explores one particular form: the college research paper. One of the mistakes students often make is assuming that college writing has no application beyond the university. In other words, it's this thing we do in school, but you'll never use those skills again. While it's true that much of what we do in college is focused on a particular kind of education, it isn't true that college writing loses its value once you graduate. The purpose of the college research paper isn't to give you a single map to cover every possible writing avenue you might stroll down in your life. Rather, the college research paper is a toolbox with a wide range of uses. This toolbox can be applied across multiple disciplines within the university and can provide a plethora of skills to be applied in everyday life.

Learning how to structure your essays can help you organize other kinds of written communication, from memos to news articles to job application materials. Learning to identify and avoid logical fallacies can help you navigate the chaotic and often bewildering world of the YouTube comments section, Facebook, or other forms of social media that might one day appear on the Internet. Most importantly, learning how to find and understand research in its myriad of forms can help you better understand the world you live in now and the world to come.

The second-to-last of these is a prime example of the value of college-level writing for civil discourse. Recognizing that it's a fallacy to attack the person instead of the argument (ad hominem) or that thesis statements need to be argumentative instead of factual are some of the things students learn as they work their way through the college world. They are also things you'll find yourself thinking about as you look at the responses to your favorite music video on YouTube or a piece of political news on Facebook or Twitter. It's a process of trial and error; the more you practice and learn, the better your writing — and thinking — will be.

Becoming a better writer — in and beyond college — can also have a profound impact on your future. In my years of teaching, I have had the honor to work with students from all walks of life and from all over the globe. So many of my students come to college having learned the formulas for good writing but still need to develop the kind of analytical and critical thinking that comes with a college education. This takes practice — and time. But learning these skills is both rewarding and crucial to your success.

Of course, so much of learning depends on you, the student. It isn't common for students to enter college writing classes in fits of joy at the word "comma" or "thesis." Teachers sometimes dream of such students, but we recognize them as a fantasy. More often than not, students enter writing classes because they have to be there. That situation poses unique challenges for teachers, especially when it comes to fostering a desire for life-long learning in students. But if you come into the classroom with an open mind, you just might find that the world of English and writing as a lot to offer. It can open doorways, change how you see the world, and even introduce you to passions you didn't know you had.

To give you an example, I'll tell you about one of my former students. He came to the United States from Venezuela in the early years of the country's recession. As an ESL (English as a Second Language) learner, he struggled to convey his ideas in the English language. Rather than let that get the best of him, he worked hard to hone his writing and argumentative skills. When he left my class, he could easily convey his arguments in his essays and in class. The last time I spoke to him, he had been accepted into a government internship program in Washington, D.C., a product, I'm sure, of his passion for civil discourse and diligent attention to detail.

Indeed, helping students find their passion for the written word is one of my goals when I teach a writing class. I consider it an enormous success if I meet a former student and learn that they're reading books, writing on the regular, and discovering new ways to engage with the written word. I also consider it a success if my students simply become better writers and use their newly developed or honed skills to move up in the world.

With that in mind, I hope you find the content of this book helpful. Use it to become a stronger writer in college. Take those skills with you wherever you go. You never know when they may come in use!

—Shaun Duke, M.A., University of Florida

Introduction

Most college students have a story of a time they procrastinated on a research paper. Maybe they stayed up all night underneath the library's weak fluorescent lights. They remember the slightly sickening taste of coffee and energy drinks at 2 a.m. They know what it feels like to stare at a computer screen, watching the cursor pulse and hearing the clock tick. They debate asking their professor for an extension, but know it will hurt their grade.

There are a lot of experiences that students want to have in college, but the staying-up-too-late-stressing-over-a-research-paper experience isn't one of those.

Of course, writing a research paper isn't easy, whether you are writing in the middle of the night on a tight deadline or if you plan in advance. A research paper — especially in college — requires using a variety of methods to learn about a topic, synthesizing information from different sources, forming your own argument based on available evidence, and presenting your ideas in a way that other people can understand.

Some students have experience writing research papers in high school; others may be entirely new to the research paper process. Regardless, college professors typically have higher expectations than high school teachers, and students may receive less guidance on their research papers. Professors are busy, and they often read hundreds of student papers for each class they teach — which makes it extra important for students to write excellent research papers that really stand out.

The 101 tips included in this book don't involve using a big font or wide margins to make your paper seem longer. They include advice on how to conduct research effectively and efficiently, how to craft an argument based on your own ideas, and how to make your writing sound impressive and professional.

Whether you consider yourself a struggling writer, a newcomer to the college writing scene, or a skilled writer looking for more ways to enhance your writing, this book can help. Writing papers does not have to involve hours of staring at a blank screen and wondering where to start. With practice, writing research papers can become simple and painless — and even a valuable learning exercise.

Chapter 1
What Is A Research Paper?

The definition of a research paper follows fairly simply from the term itself. A research paper is any paper that requires students to research — or study independently — a particular topic and present their findings in the form of an essay. The majority of papers that students write in academic settings are research papers.

The key trait of research papers is their basis in facts. Unlike opinion pieces you might read in the newspaper, research papers are not merely the author's own thoughts on a particular subject. Rather, research papers require students to back up their claims with evidence — evidence that is found by researching a certain topic.

Research papers require students to learn about a particular topic themselves, in order to write a paper about it. However, research papers aren't just about regurgitating knowledge. They typically ask students to think critically about a topic — for example, by analyzing conflicting information from different sources or by forming their own conclusions based on existing research. Because these skills can be applied in nearly any discipline, research papers are a staple in almost every subject within the academic world.

Research Papers In College

For many students, one of the most intimidating aspects of a research paper is the length. While research papers vary in length — some may only be a few pages, while others may be long enough for a book — they tend to be pretty substantial. Students often wonder: How can I fill this many pages? How can I find enough to say?

 **Tip #1**

> College research papers require you to take a nuanced approach to complicated topics — there are not simple yes or no answers.

The answer to meeting the word or page count for a particular research paper lies in the ideas. Research papers are supposed to be complicated. If a particular question could be answered with a simple "yes" or "no," a professor would not assign it as a research paper topic.

Types of research papers

There are many different types of research papers. Some research papers are short and concise, while others dive deeply into a topic. Everything from a three-page literary analysis to a 100-page senior thesis is a research paper. However, all research papers tend to follow the same basic process — whether they are summarizing research from a chemistry lab, analyzing a nineteenth-century Russian novel, or making an assessment about modern culture based on several sociological studies.

Generally, all research papers will require you to assert a thesis — the main point of the paper. You will then need to back up your thesis with evidence, such as data, quotes, theoretical examples, or other information which helps convince your reader that your thesis is correct.

In college, most research papers will require you to think beyond simply what you have learned in class. While you will likely be expected to draw on class readings or lectures in your paper, your professor certainly doesn't want your research paper to be a repetition of what they told you in class.

 *Tip #2*

Research papers require you to look up sources and explore a topic on your own. You cannot simply rely on your knowledge from class when you are writing a research paper.

The importance of timing

Since research papers require you to come up with an argument and support it with evidence, the research paper process can be divided into three main stages. First, you must figure out the main point of your paper. Second, you must gather evidence that supports this point. Finally, you must write the paper, explaining to your audience how your evidence supports your argument.

The order of these stages can sometimes vary. You may think you know the main point of your paper, but encounter evidence in your research that requires you to modify your thesis. In certain fields, such as science, your entire paper may depend on the outcome of an experiment, in which case you may have to do all your research before your start your paper. Regardless of the exact order, you will need to work on your research paper in steps — it is not something you can do in one night.

 **Tip #3**

Start your research paper well in advance of the deadline.

Time management is difficult for many college students. In addition to your research paper, you'll certainly have coursework for the rest of your classes. Many college students also work jobs, play sports, are involved with clubs, or have to help family members.

Tip #4

Set goals or draw up a schedule for when you want various stages of your project to be done.

One of the best ways to attack a research paper is by dividing it into simple steps and setting mini-deadlines for yourself. For example, decide on dates when you want to have a draft of your thesis statement, and when you want to have most of your research complete. Try to schedule your time so that you have a completed draft of your paper in advance of the deadline — that way you will have time to revise and edit.

Questions To Ask Before You Begin

Research papers are not easy. The last thing you want to do is give yourself extra work. Asking the right questions before you start working on your paper can help make the research and writing processes more efficient, saving you time and energy.

 *Tip #5*

Make sure you know the requirements of the paper before you start your research.

Many professors will give you an assignment sheet or a rubric. Read it! If you have questions, ask your professor after class, or ask via an email. The worst thing you can do to yourself is research the wrong subject, which wastes a lot of time and delays progress on your assignment.

There are several important requirements to look for when you are beginning your research paper. Most teachers will tell you the expected length of your paper. Make sure to take note of this — a five-page paper won't require as much research as a 20-page paper, so it's helpful to know which one you will be writing. There can be other requirements too. For example, your professor might ask you to use at least ten sources.

Tip #6

While you are working on your research paper, try to find time to ask your professor questions if you encounter problems along the way. Many professors hold office hours or allow you to make an appointment to discuss your ideas. Some students think that asking a lot of questions makes them seem stupid. In reality, it shows your professor or instructor that you care about succeeding.

If your professor is unavailable to help you with your paper, see if you can get assistance from a teaching assistant, a writing tutor, or a friend. Many colleges have writing centers or tutoring options that are free for students — see what resources are available at your school.

This chapter has addressed the basics of what makes a research paper and how to approach intimidating nature of research paper assignments. The next two chapters will cover how to plan your paper and conduct your research.

Chapter 2
Planning Your Paper

When assigned a research paper, some students are tempted to jump right in and begin writing. They know the assignment is big, so they don't want to waste any time. While this approach might be tempting, planning is an essential part of the writing process for this type of paper.

Planning is important because it allows you to focus your energy on what really matters for your paper. If you pick the wrong topic or come up with a weak thesis, then you end up spending time researching subjects that don't actually help you.

 *Tip #7*

When you are working on a research paper, try to do most of your research before you begin writing the actual paper.

Planning your research and the structure of your essay is essential to maintaining the academic integrity of your work. If you begin writing your paper before you've conducted your research, you risk encountering new information later that may change your stance or disprove your arguments. In this case, you must also resist the temptation to include only quotes or paraphrases that seem to support your claim, when the bulk of your research or sources disagree. Ignoring strong evidence against your argument or skewing research to better support a shaky claim is known as "cherry-picking" information, and should always be avoided.

Choosing Your Topic

Sometimes, your professor may assign you a specific research topic. In other cases, you may be asked to pick a topic yourself. Picking your own topic can be fun because you get to choose something that interests you. However, choosing your own topic also comes with some risks.

 **Tip #8**

Pick a topic that is an appropriate size given the length and time frame of the paper you are writing.

The most common mistake students make when picking a research paper topic is choosing one that is the wrong size. If you choose a topic that is too broad, you will be overwhelmed with information. At the same time, if you pick a topic that is too narrow, you might not be able to find enough information about it.

Narrowing a broad topic

Some students pick an overly broad topic, because they want to ensure they have enough material. For example, the prospect of writing a 20-page paper seems intimidating, so some students might decide to write their paper about World War II. There is certainly enough information about World War II to write a 20-page paper — but many historians have written whole books about it.

Most college research papers will require you to focus on a fairly narrow subject area. Rather than writing about World War II, you would want to focus on a particular aspect of the war. For example, pick a particular battle or political decision that was essential to the war, and write your paper about that instead.

Listen to your professor!

Even if you are picking your own topic, you should be aware of guidance from your professor. Professors will often provide a general theme for an assignment and expect students to pick a topic relating to that theme. Your professor might also name one or two topics covered within the class that should not be included in any papers. They might also have a list of topics that they see too often and recommend students avoid. Make sure to follow their instructions!

The Thesis Statement

In a research paper, your thesis statement is your central argument that you support with facts from your research. This means you have to know quite a bit about your topic before you write your thesis statement. You can't expect to know your own argument before you've done a considerable amount of research.

 *Tip #9*

> You should have a general idea of what your thesis statement will be when you start doing research — this way you don't waste your time researching ideas that are not related to your topic.

Try to come up with a thesis statement fairly early in your research. This way you can focus your research on finding evidence that supports your research, rather than generally gathering information about a topic.

 *Tip #10*

> Your thesis statement is the most important part of your research paper. The rest of your paper is all about supporting your thesis.

Thesis statement formulas

Your thesis statement is the most important part of your paper. That might sound like a lot of pressure, but the good news is that your thesis statement will be short. Most are only a few sentences.

> Although the thesis statement is short, it should not be neglected. Many students make the mistake of rushing through their thesis rather than thinking critically about their ideas. A weak thesis statement is difficult to support, while a strong thesis statement sets the foundation for a strong paper.

A good thesis statement has several key characteristics. First, a good thesis statement is true, or at the very least supported by evidence. Second, a good thesis statement must be arguable. The statement "water boils at 100 degrees Celsius" cannot be a thesis statement because it is not debatable. All scientific evidence indicates that water boils at 100 degrees Celsius — a paper with this thesis statement would be very boring!

Most thesis statements follow the same basic formula: "This is true for these reasons." You state your main point and describe, in a very general way, the reasons why that main point is true. The true assertion in your thesis statement shouldn't be any old fact. It should contain your original ideas about your topic, which you developed in the research process.

Your thesis statement should use formal language. You want to sound professional. However, don't go crazy with a thesaurus because you're trying to sound smart. Never use a word in your thesis statement (or anywhere else in your paper) if you don't know what it means.

Example thesis statements

No one writes a perfect thesis statement on the first try. When writing your thesis statement, it's helpful to begin with your topic, determine what your argument is and then provide a brief overview of your evidence. Initial drafts of your thesis statement can be informal, and are just to help you figure out your ideas. The following examples show the development of thesis statements.

Example research topic: Is preschool important for children?

> *Beginning thesis statement:* Children who go to preschool are likely to turn out better in life.

This thesis statement isn't awful. It tells the reader that your paper will be addressing how preschool impacts children in their future. However, this thesis statement is quite vague. The phrase "turn out better in life" can be interpreted in many ways, and doesn't show very much thoughtfulness or academic rigor. Try to make your thesis statement more specific.

Revised thesis statement: Research indicates that children who attend preschool have better outcomes throughout the rest of their educational careers.

This thesis statement is an improvement. It addresses the specific evidence about preschool and children's education outcomes and provides your reader with a better understanding of what to expect in your paper. However, this thesis statement still has room to develop. The thesis statement is fairly basic — in fact, it is repeating the ideas of other researchers who have found that preschool helps children. In college, you are expected not just to cite sources to support your claims, but to understand them and develop their ideas. The final thesis statement example shows how you can integrate research from many sources and create a claim of your own.

Final thesis statement: Research has repeatedly shown that children who attend preschool get better grades and are more likely to graduate high school than their counterparts. Therefore, providing universal access to preschool should be a priority for education policymakers.

This final thesis statement is the best of the three because it includes an original argument. Based on the research that preschool improves children's outcomes, the paper will argue that it is important for all children to have the chance to attend preschool. This is a subjective claim, but the writer will use evidence to back it up. Thus, this is a strong thesis for a research paper.

Example research topic: What is the meaning of Fyodor Dostoyevsky's *Crime and Punishment?*

Beginning thesis statement: Fyodor Dostoyevsky's 19th-century novel *Crime and Punishment* addresses the subject of religion.

This thesis statement is a good place to begin. It identifies religion as an important topic in the novel. However, it doesn't provide any particular insight — most people who read *Crime and Punishment* will notice the religious references.

Revised thesis statement: The 19th-century novel *Crime and Punishment* by Fyodor Dostoyevsky uses religious references to emphasize the importance of traditional Russian values.

This thesis statement is much better. Rather than simply making an observation about the novel, it shows the reader's interpretation.

Final thesis statement: The novel *Crime and Punishment* by Fyodor Dostoyevsky uses religious references to emphasize the importance of traditional Russian values. The novel can be viewed as a pushback against the encroachment of Western ideals into Russia during the 19th century.

This final thesis statement is a strong example for a college research paper. It not only analyzes *Crime and Punishment*, but also brings in outside research to help understand the novel in its cultural context.

Ways To Organize

There's a frustrating feeling you get when you're sitting in front of your computer writing a draft of your paper, and you can't remember a particular fact. Maybe it's a statistic—was it 13 percent or 31? Maybe it's a quote — you remember finding this incredible quote about religion in *Crime in Punishment* that totally supports your thesis, but you can't remember where you read it.

 **Tip #11**

> Write down important information in your notes — don't count on yourself to remember everything!

You can avoid many problems if you take good notes while you are researching. Taking research notes is different than taking notes in class. You're probably used to taking notes while your teacher talks, but your research notes require you to think about information from many different sources. You'll need to adjust your note-taking strategies.

One way to organize your research is by dividing your topic into smaller categories. Pick a mechanism for keeping track of each category, and sort all of your information accordingly. For example, some people like to use colored note cards to keep track of research. They might have four colors of note cards for their four categories. When they find a new fact, they write it on a note card of the corresponding color.

➤ Tip #12

Sort your information within your notes.

Many students like to take notes or keep track of information on their computers. That's OK too. You can consider sorting your information using different documents, different colored fonts, or another system that works best for you.

For example, let's say you're writing about Dostoyevsky's 19th-century novel *Crime and Punishment*. First, you want to consider the historical context for the novel, including biographical information about Dostoyevsky and facts about Russia at the time the novel was written. Second, you'll want to analyze the novel itself — specifically quotes or references that support your point. This arrangement would give you two categories of information.

➤ Tip #13

Make sure to keep track of where your information comes from. Knowing which sources provided you with which material will be important when it is time for citations, and it makes it easier for you to go back and look up facts later.

When you are sorting information into categories, make sure you still know the information's original source. If the information comes from a book, write down the title of the book, the author, and the page number. If it comes from the internet, write down the URL address. If it comes from a different source (a documentary, an interview, or something else), make sure you write down enough that you can figure out later where the facts came from.

Keeping track of where your information comes from makes it easier for you to check your facts later, and it helps ensure you avoid plagiarism, which will be discussed in greater depth in Chapter 5.

Brainstorming and prewriting

Once you have gathered information and figured out your argument, the next step is turning the facts in your notes into a cohesive research paper. Brainstorming helps you make connections between your ideas and get yourself ready to write. If you've been having trouble drawing a conclusion from your research in order to form a thesis statement, the connections you make between ideas while brainstorming might help clarify your main point for you.

Freewriting

One brainstorming technique is known as freewriting. With freewriting, you give yourself a particular amount of time to write down whatever comes to mind about your topic. Because you are writing, you will naturally try to convert your ideas into some sort of narrative, and you might think of things while you are writing that will help with your paper.

You can do a freewrite either by hand or on your computer. When you are freewriting, don't worry about spelling or grammar. Just think about your ideas. The following is a sample freewrite about the novel *Crime and Punishment*.

Dostoyevsky wrote the novel in 1866, during a time when many ideas were spreading around Europe. Raskolnikov, the protagonist, is rather intellectual, and commits the murder to test his own philosophical theories. Afterwards, he compares himself to Napoleon. However, Raskolnikov is not the superman-like figure that he thought he could be. He ends up being wracked by guilt over his actions before confessing to Sonya, who is a religious figure in the novel. Raskolnikov only achieves solitude after turning himself in and spending time in prison, therefore paying for his sins. This shows the role of religion in the novel.

Mind mapping

Mind mapping is another useful brainstorming technique. Mind mapping lets you draw connections between subjects visually. If you're artistic, you can even break out your colored pencils or rulers. For a mind map, start with your general topic area in the middle of your paper, and branch out, connecting other topics as you go. Don't hold back — exercises like mind-mapping work best when you just let the ideas flow and connect.

If you prefer to use your computer, you can still create a mind map digitally; there are many online programs that you can use. Check out sites like MindMup (**www.mindmup.com**) and Free Mind (**http://freemind .sourceforge.net**).

Outlining

The most common brainstorming and organization technique is outlining. When outlining, you draft a condensed, bullet-pointed version of your paper that establishes your main ideas and the order they might go in. Your outline might start with your thesis statement and include a few bullet points for each of your main subjects.

A short research paper might only need a brief outline or flowchart to help you remember the order of your key points. Long research papers or scientific dissertations might require a more detailed outline to stay on track. Just as there is no wrong way to prewrite, there is no wrong way to write an outline for a paper as long as it gets the job done. Try different outlines, and see which helps you with your writing process the most.

The following is an example of a basic topic outline about *Crime and Punishment*:

> *Thesis Statement:* The novel *Crime and Punishment* by Fyodor Dostoyevsky uses religious references to emphasize the importance of traditional Russian values. The novel can be viewed as a push-back against the encroachment of Western ideals into Russia during the 19th century.

1. Raskolnikov commits murder to test his philosophical theories.

    -He is a former student.

    -He justifies himself by saying that the woman he killed was a bad person anyway.

    -He argues that he is special, and therefore won't be affected by the murder.

    -He compares himself to Napoleon.

2. He is wracked by guilt until he finds salvation through religion.

    -He starts having hallucinations and feels very guilty.

    -He first confesses to Sonya, who supports him.

    -He ultimately turns himself in to face tangible punishment, eventually leading to his redemption.

3. Raskolnikov's journey reflects competing ideas in Europe during the 19th century.

-When Raskolnikov murders, he is relying on Western philosophical ideas.

-His philosophy proves wrong, as shown by his guilt.

-He starts to improve through his relationship with Sonya, which represents a return to traditional Russia.

-He ultimately achieves salvation, but only after going to prison and paying for his sins.

Brainstorming is an essential part of the research paper process. You don't have to try every brainstorming activity, but it's a good idea to try something. You can also mix and match — create a mind map or freewrite to get yourself thinking, and then make an outline once your ideas are more developed.

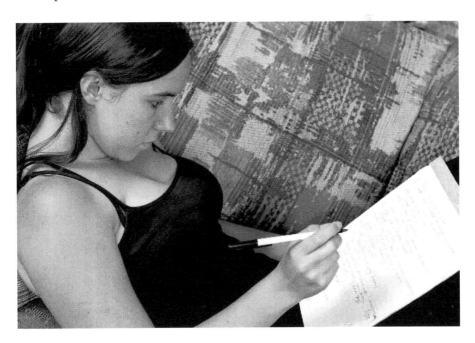

Knowing how to organize your ideas is important, but it is important to do your research so you have good ideas in the first place. The next chapter will address research methods, so you can gather enough information to write your paper.

Chapter 3
Beginning Your Research

Once you have a narrow topic and a good idea where you want to go with it, it is time to start researching. Research involves gathering information on your own that will help you support your thesis and write your paper.

Even if you haven't written a research paper before, you probably have conducted some research. If you've ever read a nonfiction book or looked up a fact on the internet, you've technically been doing research. Of course, these types of research are less formal and rigorous than the research you will do for a college paper. Still, with the prevalence of the internet, doing research for your paper is easier now than it has ever been.

However, research also brings its challenges. Many students struggle to find sources that address their specific research subjects. And although the internet makes it easy to access many possible sources, not all information is reliable. This chapter will provide an overview of the different kinds of sources and give you the tools to evaluate sources for bias and determine which sources are best for your paper.

What Counts As A Source?

When asked to look for sources, many students think of thick library books and dusty old documents. Obviously you shouldn't discount books or primary sources — both of these will be discussed at length later in the book — but you also shouldn't limit yourself when it comes to finding sources for your paper.

 **Tip #14**

Don't limit yourself by only using sources that you can read. Documentaries, photos, the radio, and podcasts can also be useful sources.

The number and types of sources that you will use for your research paper vary drastically based on the subject, length, and requirements of your paper. If you are writing a paper about a particular piece of literature, for example, you may primarily use that work as your main source, and only have a few other sources. By contrast, a history paper may require you to use many different sources in order to obtain different perspectives.

 **Tip #15**

Depending on your subject area, you may want to conduct a survey or interviews for your research paper.

Conducting an experiment

In college, research papers will typically ask you to draw some sort of original conclusion about your topic. Your professors are experts in their field — if your research paper simply regurgitates arguments that other students or academics have made, your professor will certainly recognize them. One way to come up with an original argument for your paper is by designing your own specific experiment.

Tip #16

Many research papers in the sciences or social sciences may require you to conduct your own experiment and then write a research paper about it. If you need to conduct your own experiment, make sure to plan ahead.

If you are designing your own experiment for a research paper, it is a good idea to consult your professor beforehand. Experiments take a lot of time and energy, so you want to make sure you are on the right track.

Primary, Secondary, and Tertiary Sources

There are three kinds of sources: primary, secondary, and tertiary. Of these three types, tertiary sources are the most general. Tertiary sources refer to encyclopedias, atlases, or other reference books that you might use at the very beginning of your research. These sources might provide you with basic background information, help you come up with keywords for further research, or direct you to other sources. Because they provide such basic information, tertiary sources should not make up the bulk of your research.

Tip #17

Tertiary sources, such as encyclopedias, are a good way to introduce yourself to a topic that you don't know very well.

Secondary sources are sources written by other researchers who have studied the same topic as you. Textbooks, biographies, and journal articles are a few examples of secondary sources. People who write secondary sources typically write them by examining primary and other secondary sources.

Primary sources are firsthand accounts of information without additional interpretation. They include raw research data from experiments, original works of fiction, statistics, interviews, letters, diaries, photographs, eyewitness accounts, and many government records. Don't use a work of fiction as a primary source unless you're writing about that work, its genre, or its creator. For example, Steven Spielberg's movie *Lincoln* is not a credible source for your paper about Abraham Lincoln. It is, however, a credible source for a paper about Steven Spielberg's film techniques.

 ► *Tip #18*

Many primary sources, such as old photographs or newspaper clippings, are now digitized and available online. The Library of Congress (loc.gov) and the National Archives (archives.gov) are good places to start looking for primary sources pertaining to American history.

The Purpose Of Sources

An academic journal article, a YouTube video, a blog post, a news article, an e-book, and a book you find in the library — all of these might serve as sources for a research paper. The key to writing a strong paper isn't just knowing how to find good sources, but knowing how to use different types of sources in different ways.

 **Tip #19**

> Nearly anything can be a source for a college research paper — but only if used the right way.

If you are writing a paper for your chemistry class about a particular scientific concept, you want to make sure your information is scientifically accurate. A journal article written by an actual scientist makes a good source, while a random blog post on the internet is less likely to have correct information. On the other hand, if you're writing a paper about the growing problem of scientific misinformation on the internet, you might cite a random blog post as an example.

When you are finding sources, always make sure to ask yourself this question: What would my professor think of this source? A children's book about chemistry might be a useful source for a paper about teaching elementary education, but it would be inappropriate for a college-level science paper. Some classes and topics might require more formal sources whereas some professors might be comfortable allowing you to use blogs and comic strips as part of your research. On the opposite end of the spectrum, sources that are too technical might be inappropriate.

Always make sure that you fully understand your sources. Some sources might be above the level of research expected for the project you are working on, which can be just as bad as using sources that are too simplistic. If a source is so full of jargon that you can't understand it, you probably won't use it properly. Make sure every source you use fits the type of paper you are writing.

Evaluating sources

When evaluating sources, you want to look for a few key traits. First, sources with authors listed are always more reliable. If a source has an author, it means that a person is accountable for the information provided.

If a source has an author listed, you can use the internet to look up their qualifications. You can check if they have a personal website, if they appear on sites like LinkedIn, if they have written for other reputed publications before, or if they are listed on the websites of reputable organizations.

Learning about the author can certainly help you decide whether to trust a source. For example, you may come across a scientific article on the internet and be unsure as to whether it is reliable. However, if you discover that the author is a highly qualified scientist, then you can probably trust it.

Tip #20

Try to double-check important facts with multiple sources. If many sources give you the same information, there is a higher probability that the information is true than if you only found it in one source.

It is always a good idea to use multiple sources to crosscheck information during your research. If multiple sources contain similar information, that information is more likely to be accurate. On the other hand, if you find that several different sources provide conflicting information on a particular issue, you should make sure to research it further to figure out what is correct. Don't just pick the source that best supports your point.

► *Tip #21*

Some articles and journals are peer-reviewed, which means a team of experts on the subject examined the contents and possibly revised them. Look for peer-reviewed sources — their information is likely to be accurate.

Sometimes, experts have already done the fact checking for you. A peer-reviewed journal article is a type of research paper that is written by college and graduate school professors and other experts. These papers undergo thorough editing and fact checking by other researchers before they are published. Look for peer-reviewed articles — they are likely to be reliable.

► *Tip #22*

Check the date on the source you are using—if you are dealing with a contemporary subject, make sure your information isn't outdated.

When you are fact checking, you should also always check the date of your sources. Science and technology, for example, have made a lot of progress in recent years. If you are looking at a scientific paper from many years ago, you might want to see if there are more recent papers that support or contradict your old source.

Biased sources

Bias refers to an author's tendency to promote a particular point of view. A source might be biased if the author intentionally misleads the reader or omits key information in order to make a point. But bias doesn't have to be malicious — some authors are biased simply because of the way they experience the world.

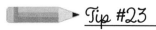

Tip #23

Even if sources are factually correct, they can still exhibit bias.

When you are investigating a source's author, you should consider what associations or affiliations the author might have. For example, if an author who is writing about the connection between fossil fuels and climate change is also employed by an oil company, their job might pose a conflict of interest and cause bias in their work.

Your evaluation of a source's reliability and bias shouldn't be based on the author alone. Someone without formal education can still conduct good research — that's why it's a good idea to examine what (if any) sources an author cites. If an author has acquired their information from reliable sources, they are likely to have created a reliable source too.

> Regardless of the author, you should evaluate the source yourself for bias. Certain keywords can tip you off that a source might be exhibiting substantial bias.

Watch out for vague or non-specific language, as it allows authors to argue weak claims without being technically wrong. For example, the word "many" is meaningless in a research paper. If the author says "many people" believe something, they could mean that 10 people believe it, or 50, or 500,000. Authors might use language like this when they really have no idea what the actual number is — don't be fooled. Likewise, be wary of authors who say "studies show" or "the data indicate" without listing any studies or data to back up their claims.

Finally, watch out for authors who use strong or loaded language. Trust your instincts — if the tone of a piece seems angry, or overly positive, or overtly leaning to one side, it's probably biased.

 ► *Tip #24*

A source can have bias but still be useful. Biased primary sources might explain an individual's motivations or intentions. Make sure that you remain an objective researcher and you consider the source's bias when you are writing your paper.

Once again, it's important to consider the purpose of a source when you are writing your research paper. For example, an article written by a political candidate about his economic plan might not be a reliable source about the state of the economy. But it might be a useful source if you are writing a paper about economic motivations and political movements.

Where To Look

Given the widespread availability of technology, there are many ways to do research. This can be overwhelming — where do you even start? A college or university library can be a good place to begin, if you have access to one.

Although it's possible to find sources online, it's good to start your research at a library. Libraries have encyclopedias and reference books to help you gather background information. They likely have books specific to your topic, and librarians who are trained to help you with your research, too.

Libraries often have another important tool — access to archives and databases. Libraries often subscribe to journals and magazines, and have copies going back many years. Although some students think they can find everything on the internet, that's simply not true. Don't limit yourself and your research by sticking close to your computer.

Books are great

The internet may be a more popular form of research now, but books are an incredibly important resource. Unlike internet sources, books typically undergo a thorough editing and fact checking process, so they are likely to be reliable.

➤ Tip #25

Reading several books on your subject matter can be daunting, especially if you are busy. Use the Table of Contents in a book to figure out which parts will be most relevant for you, and read those first.

Some students are overwhelmed by books — it's much easier to read a two-page article than a 250-page book. However, a book is likely to have much more information than a single article. If you only read short articles about your topic, you might miss out on the bigger picture. Books are likely to tell a complete story or narrative.

 *Tip #30*

> Wikipedia is not a reliable source, but that doesn't mean it can't be a useful one. Wikipedia pages usually have in-line citations and suggestions for further reading at the bottom of the page. These are usually good sources — look them up yourself!

Other informal websites should likewise be avoided when you are doing research. Sites like Facebook or Twitter might not seem sketchy — you might use them every day — but they don't make good sources for a research paper. It's too easy for people to create fake profiles or falsify posts, so it's really not a good idea to use social media content as a source.

Although some areas of the internet aren't good for research, you can find reliable sources on the internet if you know where to look.

 **Tip #31**

Use Google Scholar (scholar.google.com) to search for academic articles on your subject area.

Tip #32

.edu and .gov sources are the most likely to contain accurate information, as they come from colleges and universities or the U.S. government.

As with any source, it's especially important to check internet sources for bias. Avoid anonymously sourced articles, and use good judgment. If an article on the internet seems intentionally vague or makes far-fetched claims without truly backing them up, don't trust it.

Tip #33

If the source you are reading on the internet has an author listed, look up that person and see what you can find. If he or she is an expert on the subject, then your source is probably reliable, even if it was published on a .com site.

Still, the internet is an incredibly valuable resource. Many smart people — including college professors, scientific experts, and Nobel Prize winners — publish their writings on the internet all the time. As long as you research carefully, you can find the good stuff on the internet, without getting lost amongst unreliable sources.

Tip #34

If you have access to a printer, print the sources that you find on the internet. This way, you can make notes directly on the source itself. Plus, if something goes wrong with the internet or the site you used, you can still access your source.

Unlike a physical book that sits in front of you, there is greater room for problems when you are using internet sources. Always make sure to keep track of where you get your information from on the internet — this will be important when it comes time to cite your sources.

At some point, you'll need to finish the research stage of your project and start writing. For some people, it can be difficult to move on. When you conduct a lot of research, you often realize that there is a vast world out there full of things that you don't know. It can be difficult to accept that you have enough material and move on. The next chapter will look at the next stage of your research paper: turning facts and information into your own argument.

Chapter 4
Constructing Your Argument

The previous chapter discussed how to conduct research — how to gather information for your paper using a variety of sources. Research is important. Your paper needs it. But research papers aren't simply a list of facts.

A good college research paper will go beyond simply repeating information that you have acquired during your research. Critical thinking is essential to succeeding in college, and writing a research paper means that you have to think deeply about your topic. You have to consider all the information you acquire and figure out how to present it in an original and intelligent manner. This chapter will address how to make sense of your research and construct your argument, so that you can put yourself on a good path as you begin writing your paper.

Your Thesis And Beyond

Chapter 2 talked about thesis statements. As you remember, your thesis statement is your paper's central argument, summarized in a few sentences. Your thesis statement should reflect your own ideas and conclusions based on your research. The rest of your paper is all about supporting your thesis statement.

 Tip #35

Consider how the evidence from your research supports your thesis.

As you conduct your research, you should think about how new evidence relates to your thesis statement. Some information might provide important context to help your readers understand your thesis, or understand why it matters. Some evidence might directly support part of your thesis. Other evidence might contradict your thesis, and you must think about how to consider it.

Using evidence

Evidence for your research paper can take many different forms. Numerical data, quotes from experts, summaries of events, and your own observations can all serve as evidence for a research paper, depending on your subject matter and your thesis. A good researcher will be able to bring information from a variety of sources into their paper.

 *Tip #36*

Try to weave a narrative between information from different sources.

The pros and cons of data

Data is an essential part of many research papers. Some research papers, particularly in the sciences, may be almost entirely based on the data collected during a particular study. But data also comes up in other subjects. For example, a political science paper might look at the approval rate of a certain policy, or a sociology paper might analyze how many people are impacted by a particular cultural phenomenon.

Researchers like using data because it makes them seem smart. People like reading papers with data because it sounds concrete and conclusive. If a paper warns that a hurricane "could affect a lot of people," the reader might think about the possibility of a hurricane. But if a paper states that "there is an 80 percent chance of a Category 5 hurricane hitting a city with 12 million people during the next 3 months," the reader is likely to be much more concerned.

Data is undoubtedly powerful, which is why it is extra important that you, as a researcher, use it properly. When incorporating data into your paper, you should consider two key factors: accuracy and context.

Accuracy refers to how correct your data actually is. Although people think that data is objective and factual, data measurements aren't always perfect. Science students know that their measuring instruments often come with a small degree of uncertainty, and they take this into account when writing about the results of their experiments.

Data collected by other people will have inaccuracies, too. For example, many firms regularly conduct surveys of political opinions in the United States, but they all come up with slightly different results. As a researcher, you might consider looking at the results of several different polls and taking an average. Or, you might research each of the polls and decide which one uses the best methodology, and then rely on its results. Either of these methods would be better than picking a poll at random.

If your data include estimates, you should do your best to evaluate those estimates for accuracy. You may not know enough to evaluate them perfectly, but you can certainly do more research. For example, if you are researching hurricanes, you might come across a scientist whose data indicates there is an 80 percent chance of a massive hurricane hitting Miami soon. To evaluate whether this estimate is accurate, you can look at the scientist's methodology: does it make sense to you? You can also see what other scientists have said about this research. Did they support it? Or did they say this particular scientist was crazy?

In addition to considering the accuracy of a particular dataset, it is also important to weigh context when you are using data in your paper. Without proper context, your data will likely be meaningless to your reader.

For example, if you are citing a statistic in your paper about the cost of rice in Thailand, you don't want to assume that your reader knows a lot about Thai money. Rather than simply saying that a kilogram of rice costs 400 Thai baht, you want to inform your reader that this amount is equivalent to about $12. You might provide additional context for your reader by sharing data on the average monthly income of a Thai family or the costs of other foods, depending on the purpose of your paper.

Quotes

Quotes are another staple of the college research paper. They are a useful way to incorporate information from sources. If you are quoting a source, you know you must be representing it accurately. However, students frequently fall into several traps with quotes, which hurt their effectiveness.

First, it's important to avoid over-quoting in your paper. Each quote in your paper should be surrounded by several sentences of analysis. Otherwise, your paper starts to feel like a list of other people's ideas, which you are directly quoting! Furthermore, you should generally try to keep quotes in your paper short. If you use a quote that is more than four lines long, you must format it separately as a block quote. Block quotes stand alone as their own paragraph, and are indented. The details of formatting and citing quotes will be addressed more specifically in Chapter 6.

> Another mistake students make is including quotes that are highly technical or full of jargon. If you include a quote in your paper, you need to fully understand it. If the quote contains language that your reader might not know, you need to provide additional explanation.

In addition to using quotes, you will likely want to sometimes take information from sources without directly quoting them. Methods of paraphrasing and summarizing sources will be addressed in the next chapter.

➤ *Tip #37*

Make sure your argument is not based too heavily on any one source. If so, it is not really your argument — you are just restating what someone else has already said.

Your own analysis

While finding evidence to support your thesis is important, your research paper should also include your own analysis. Some students are scared to bring their own ideas into a paper. After all, it seems easier to rely on quotes and data that other people have come up with. However, your professor will likely want to see you tie together this research with your own thoughts. This analysis can happen in a few different ways.

In some classes, particularly in the social sciences, you may find it useful to examine real-world examples through theory from your discipline. For example, for an economics paper, you might show how an economic theory you have learned in class can be applied to a case study of a supermarket in your town. For a psychology paper, you could apply Freudian theory about sexuality to an analysis of online dating.

In each of these cases, your paper would rely on data — about a supermarket or online dating — and theory. Your analysis would be tying these concepts together. Does the economic theory accurately predict what will happen at the supermarket? What can Freud teach us about online dating? Answering these questions would be doing your own analysis.

Organizing your research

Organization is essential to a research paper. Just having lots of information isn't enough — you must present your ideas and your evidence in a logical order so that your reader can understand your thesis.

 *Tip #38*

> Use an outline to organize your research before you begin writing. Think about the order of your ideas and which evidence (and which sources) you will use to support each idea.

Chapter 2 discussed using an outline to help develop your ideas. As you conduct your research, your outline can become more detailed. Think about which specific pieces of evidence support which parts of your thesis, and update your planning to reflect this. Remember, the purpose of your paper is to support your thesis.

Background

Background information can be a vexing topic for many students who are writing research papers. On one hand, it is important to include enough background information so that your reader can understand your thesis. For example, if you are writing about a historical event, you probably want to provide some information about the era or the events leading up to the main event. Without this context, your reader will be confused.

On the other hand, many professors believe that students often spend too much time on background information. For example, if you are writing your research paper on a book that you read for your class, you should not waste time summarizing the entire book in your paper. Your professor probably read the book — they don't need a summary.

 *Tip #39*

Include background information — but only when it is relevant to your thesis.

When deciding what background information to include in your paper, it is useful to start with your thesis statement and work backwards. For example, if your thesis statement says that Marxian political philosophy can help us understand modern debates about the minimum wage, you probably want to provide background information about Marx's political philosophy. If your reader doesn't understand the Marxist theories that your research paper is relying on, they will likely struggle to follow your conclusions. However, this research paper would not need to include background about Karl Marx's biographical information, because it is not relevant to the thesis.

As a general rule, you can always exclude background information that is considered common knowledge. For example, if you are writing a paper about the U.S. Constitution, you do not need to remind your reader that the United States was founded in 1776 after declaring its independence from Great Britain. However, if you were writing a paper about the government of the Republic of Moldova, it would be more important to include background information — because an understanding of the Moldovan government is not considered common knowledge at most American colleges.

Considering Alternative Perspectives

One of the biggest challenges during the research paper process is dealing with conflicting information. Research papers address complicated topics

— you are bound to find different perspectives. The key to a good paper is acknowledging that other viewpoints exist while still arguing for your thesis.

 *Tip #40*

Make sure to read sources that have an alternative perspective from your thesis. Be prepared to acknowledge or respond to these arguments in your paper.

When you encounter conflicting evidence

Conflicting evidence comes in many forms during your research. At times, you will find that sources disagree over basic facts. These conflicts are not necessarily mistakes — even experts come to different conclusions some time. For example, some sources say that there were 28,000 Confederate casualties at the Battle of Gettysburg, while others say that there were only 23,000. In this case, these distinctions are fairly minor. The conclusion of your research paper likely won't change based on which number you use.

In other cases, you might find that experts disagree not just on numbers, but on ideas as well. For example, historians have different thoughts about the significance of the Battle of Gettysburg in the context of the Civil War. If you are writing your paper about the impact of the Battle of Gettysburg on the remaining course of the Civil War, your thesis will likely agree with some historians and disagree with others.

Depending on the subject matter, you might take a position that strongly agrees with some experts, and disagrees with others. You might take a position that falls somewhere in the middle. Or you may even come up with an innovative argument that reconciles some of the differences among experts and presents an entirely new conclusion, which is entirely your own.

The following examples show different ways that you could address conflicting evidence in your research paper.

> While historians dispute the exact number of Confederate soldiers who died during the Battle of Gettysburg, most agree that it was around 25,000.

> Although some historians have argued that Fyodor Dostoyevsky's time in prison inspired *Crime and Punishment*, the novel is actually more of a reflection of Dostoyevsky's philosophical ideas than his own experiences.

> Some psychologists have argued that online dating is fundamentally detrimental to human relationships because it leads to objectification and reinforces the desire for instant gratification. However, others argue that online dating extends previous courtship rituals, only with more options because of technology. Ultimately, the truth lies somewhere in between. While objectification has existed for centuries, online dating does speed up the courtship process, and therefore can be damaging to interpersonal relationships.

For many students, the worst part of conflicting evidence is the fear it creates. Students worry that they are picking the wrong side, and that their whole paper will fail as a result. Try to avoid this type of thinking! Generally, the point of research papers is to show off your research and critical thinking skills. As long as you establish a thesis and support it with strong evidence, you will be fine. Acknowledging the existence of alternative perspectives shows your reader that you have done thorough research and that you understand that the world is complicated. It is not something to be scared of.

This chapter has discussed how to use evidence to support your thesis, how to develop your own analysis, and how to deal with alternative perspectives during the research process. If you have addressed these topics during your own research and planning, you are probably ready to begin writing a draft of your own paper. Good luck!

Chapter 5
Avoiding Plagiarism

You've probably heard of plagiarism, a form of cheating that happens when students try to cut corners on research papers or similar assignments. When students are caught for plagiarism, they sometimes try to claim that they didn't understand what plagiarism was, and they didn't know their actions were wrong.

This chapter will give a clear overview of what constitutes plagiarism. You will understand why plagiarism is such a problem in academia, and you will know how to avoid it when writing your own paper — thus staying out of trouble and giving people credit for work that is rightfully theirs.

What Is Plagiarism?

The Merriam-Webster Dictionary defines plagiarism as "the act of using another person's words or ideas without giving credit to that person." Essentially, plagiarism is made up of two crimes. First, people who plagiarize steal the work of another person. Second, they lie about it by failing to give credit.

So what makes plagiarism different from quoting or using information from other sources? After all, you have learned that you are supposed to rely on information from other sources for your research paper.

Your work becomes plagiarism if you fail to acknowledge the sources you used. For example, the paragraph at the beginning of this section quoted from the Merriam-Webster dictionary. This is not plagiarism. The sentence makes it clear that the paragraph uses a quote — it is in quotation marks and is directly attributed to Merriam-Webster. Additionally, the Merriam-Webster page is cited in the bibliography of this book.

If the section had opened "Plagiarism is the act of using another person's words or ideas without giving credit to that person," with no acknowledgement of where that definition came from, then it would have been plagiarism.

Plagiarism isn't limited to copying from online sources. The following sections will explore a few other common instances of plagiarism and how to avoid them.

 ► *Tip #41*

Most colleges and universities have strict policies about plagiarism. You can probably look up your school's rules about plagiarism online or in a student handbook.

Obvious plagiarism

Some forms of plagiarism are obvious. It is plagiarism to submit work written by anyone else; you can't borrow an essay that an older student wrote in the past. Asking a friend to write any part of your paper for you is plagiarism too. Even if a particular part of your paper is really tough, you have to write it yourself.

It is OK to have a friend, tutor, or family member look at your paper and give suggestions. However, they shouldn't write any parts of your paper for you. For example, it is fine if your friend tells you, "This sentence doesn't make sense. You should rewrite it." However, your friend cannot rewrite the sentence for you.

Failing to properly cite information is also plagiarism. If a source helps with your paper in any capacity, you must include it in a works cited or bibliography page. Specific facts, like quotes, paraphrases, summaries, and statistics, typically require you to use inline citations, which will be discussed later in this chapter.

 Tip #42

> If you're not sure whether you should cite something, cite it. It's better to be safe than sorry. If you are able to, ask your professor for their opinion.

Paraphrasing and summarizing

Sometimes you will encounter incredibly important information in a source, but it won't be phrased in a way that works for your paper. When this occurs, you can either paraphrase or summarize the information. Because paraphrasing and summarizing involve restating someone else's ideas in your own words, you must cite the information. If you don't cite something that you paraphrase or summarize, you have plagiarized.

 **Tip #43**

Paraphrasing should be rewriting the author's ideas in your own words, not substituting a few words in a sentence.

Let's say you're researching the impact of preschool on child development, and you come across the following passage in a research paper about child-care and behavioral development:

> *Original passage:* "Consistent with our basic hypothesis, our results overall indicate that there is a positive relation between child-care quality and preschool children's developmental outcomes across the whole variety of domains that were studied: receptive language abilities, pre-academic skills, classroom behaviors, and attitudes toward child care, and perceptions of competence. All of these are primary areas of development for preschool-age children, and, furthermore, are considered important to children's ability to be ready to learn and to succeed in school. Children's skills in understanding language and the nature of their interactions with caregivers are key components relating to children's adjustment to school and early academic success."[1]

> *Bad paraphrase example:* As the researchers hypothesized, their results showed a positive relation between child-care quality and preschool children's developmental outcomes in a variety of areas, including language abilities, pre-academic skills, classroom behavior, attitudes toward child care, and perceptions of competence.

---

1. Ellen S. Peisner-Feinberg and Margaret R. Burchinal, "Relations Between Preschool Children's Child-Care Experiences and Concurrent Development: The Cost, Quality, and Outcomes Study," *Merrill-Palmer Quarterly* 43, no. 3 (1997): 451-77. Web.

These areas are considered important to children's future success. Furthermore, children's language skills and their interactions with the people who take care of them help them better adjust to school and achieve academic success.

This paraphrase is hardly a paraphrase — it changes a few words here and there, but it doesn't rewrite the passage. Including a paraphrase like this in your research paper would constitute plagiarism, because you are practically quoting someone without attributing it as a quote.

Good paraphrase example: Researchers found that improved childcare quality resulted in better outcomes for children, both in language and academic skills as well as behavior and ability to interact with adults. All of these areas are essential to preparing children for school, and children who develop more skills during early schooling are more likely to achieve academic success.

This second paraphrase is much better. Just remember — you still have to cite this passage, because you are taking another author's idea. You didn't conduct the research on quality of childcare and children's outcomes, so you must give credit to the people who did.

➤ Tip #44

Summarizing should explain the author's ideas, but in a shorter, condensed version. As with paraphrasing, the summary should be your writing, not the author's.

While paraphrasing refers to rewriting an author's ideas in your own words, summarizing means briefly describing an author's main point. A summary of the passage from the previous example would look like the following:

Good summary example: Researchers found that improved childcare quality resulted in better developmental outcomes for children, thereby preparing them for future academic success.

As with paraphrasing, you should always cite something that you summarize, because the ideas are not your own. You should do this using inline citations, which will be discussed later in this chapter.

Quoting and misquoting

Whenever you use a quote in your paper, you must cite it — otherwise, you will be plagiarizing. Always make sure to copy and cite your quotes properly. Misquoting occurs if you incorrectly copy a quote from a source. Even if it's an accident, misquoting someone misrepresents his or her ideas. Misquoting isn't plagiarism, but it is still a big mistake.

 *Tip #45*

Be extra careful to avoid typos and mistakes when quoting from a
source.

Sometimes you might want to modify a quote to make it fit better within
the text of your paper. You are allowed to modify quotes, as long as you
indicate clearly to your reader what your modifications are.

 *Tip #46*

If you want to modify a quote, you can use ellipses (. . .) to cut out an
unimportant phrase or brackets ([]) to add or substitute a clarification.

Let's take the following passage from the novel *Crime and Punishment* by
Fyodor Dostoyevsky:

> Raskolnikov had a terrible dream. He dreamed of his childhood,
> while still in their little town. He is about seven years old and is
> strolling with his father on a feast day, towards evening, outside of
> town. The weather is gray, the day is stifling, the countryside is
> exactly as it was preserved in his memory: it was even far more ef-
> faced in his memory that it appeared now in his dream. The town
> stands open to view; there is not a single willow tree around it;
> somewhere very far off, at the very edge of the sky, is the black line
> of a little forest. (54)

You want to incorporate this quote into your paper, but it's a little long.
You can cut it down using an ellipsis, as shown in the following example:

"Raskolnikov had a terrible dream. He dreamed of his childhood . . . the countryside is exactly as it was preserved in his mem-

ory: it was even far more effaced in his memory that it appeared now in his dream. The town stands open to view; there is not a single willow tree around it; somewhere very far off, at the very edge of the sky, is the black line of a little forest," (54).

Consequences of plagiarism

Students who commit plagiarism face serious consequences. In college, a student who plagiarizes may be suspended for multiple semesters, or even face expulsion. In the academic world after college, people who plagiarize have their careers forever tarnished.

> You might wonder, "If I just mess up with a sentence or two, will I really be caught?" You might be. Professors now have access to many computer programs that can quickly run through a paper and see if its content matches up with other papers, books, and internet sources. But even if your instructor doesn't choose to use such software, you should avoid plagiarism simply because it's wrong. You shouldn't take ideas from another person without giving them credit.

In the long run, plagiarizing hurts students, too. If you plagiarize your paper, you won't learn as much about the topic. You won't be forced to think critically, and you won't improve your research and writing skills.

Citation Styles

Avoiding plagiarism isn't that hard, it just requires citing your sources. When you are writing a research paper, you will typically cite your sources in two ways. You will write a bibliography or a works cited page, which will list all the sources that helped you write the paper. You will also include inline citations, also called in-text citations, in the form of footnotes, endnotes, or parenthetical citations, to specifically mark quotes and places where you paraphrased or summarized a source. Inline citations allow a reader to match something you cited with its full works-cited or bibliography entry at the end of the paper.

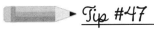 *Tip #47*

> There are many different styles of citations. The most common are MLA (typically used when writing about literature), Turabian (typically used when writing about history), and APA (typically used when writing about science). Make sure you know which citation style your instructor wants you to use.

The next few sections will show how to do inline citations in MLA, Turabian, and APA format. To learn the details of citing different types of sources in each of these styles for your bibliography or works cited, you should refer to style guides, which are available online.

 *Tip #48*

> Several websites claim to provide citation generators, which allow you to enter information and create the citation for you. However, these generators are prone to mistakes. You are better off looking up citation guides and doing the citations yourself.

MLA style

MLA format is most commonly used for papers about literature. It uses parenthetical in-text citations. Parenthetical means your citation will be enclosed with parentheses. Inside the parentheses, include the last name of the author, followed by the page number that the cited information came from. If you are writing about poetry, use the line number rather than a page number. Do not place a comma between the author's last name and the page number.

The citation should also go at the end of the information cited but before the terminal punctuation, which is usually a period. In the cases of particularly short papers or literary analysis not involving any secondary sources, you might only use one source for your paper. In this case, you can use just a page number within the parentheses.

Here are three sample citations from three different sources. A quote taken from page 15 of John Doe's book *Why Getting Citations Right is Really Important* would be presented as follows:

"There is no excuse for getting a citation wrong," (Doe 15).

If this quote came from a scholarly journal rather than a book, the parenthetical citation would look exactly the same:

"There is no excuse for getting a citation wrong," (Doe 15).

If the quote came from a website, you wouldn't have to use a page number, because websites don't have page numbers. Instead, the citation would look as follows:

"There is no excuse for getting a citation wrong," (Doe).

If Doe's book were the only source you were citing in your research paper, you wouldn't have to include his name. In that case, you would only list the page number:

"There is no excuse for getting a citation wrong," (15).

APA style

APA style has many similarities with MLA, but it comes from the American Psychological Association. It is most commonly used in psychology and the social sciences, though you might run into it in other science classes as well.

> Like MLA, APA style uses parenthetical in-text citations. However, APA includes the author's last name and the year the piece was published, with a comma in between. If you are using a quote, APA also requires you to include the page number. However, if you are just citing general information, the page number is not necessary.

The following sample citations are presented in APA format. They revolve around the same quote taken from page 15 of John Doe's book *Why Getting Citations Right is Really Important*, published in 2011. If you are quoting the passage exactly, the citation would be presented as follows:

"There is no excuse for getting a citation wrong," (Doe, 2011, pg. 15).

However, if you are paraphrasing Doe's idea, the page number would not be necessary, as shown in the next example:

Students never have a good excuse for incorrectly citing something, (Doe, 2011).

If the quote came from a website, the publication year would be the year the website was last updated. If this information is not available, use the abbreviation "n.d." to signify "no date."

"There is no excuse for getting a citation wrong," (Doe, n.d.).

Turabian/Chicago style

The third major citation style is Turabian, which is sometimes referred to as Chicago Manual or Chicago Style. Although the two styles have some subtle differences, they are almost identical, and some people use the terms interchangeably. Kate Turabian originally developed the Turabian Style for the University of Chicago. It is based on the Chicago Manual of Style (CMS), but focuses more specifically on writing college papers, theses, and dissertations.

This style is more confusing than MLA or APA because it can use either parenthetical citations or footnotes depending on the situation. There is no rule for which papers use parenthetical references and which use footnotes, so be sure to ask your professor which format you should use.

The parenthetical citations that Turabian uses are a cross between MLA and APA citations. They include a publication date, a page number, and the author's last name. The author's last name will come first followed by the year and then the page number. There is not a comma between the author's last name and the date, but there is a comma between the date and the page number.

The following sample citations are presented in Chicago format. The quote from page 15 of John Doe's 2011 book *Why Getting Citations Right is Really Important* would be presented as follows:

"There is no excuse for getting a citation wrong," (Doe 2011, 15).

If the source was journal article with the same publication year and pagination, it would be identical:

"There is no excuse for getting a citation wrong," (Doe 2011, 15).

If the source comes from a website, again use the abbreviation "n.d." to signify "no date." With websites, you do not need to use page numbers. If the source came from an undated website, it would look as follows:

"There is no excuse for getting a citation wrong," (Doe n.d.).

If you are using footnotes, insert a footnote where you would like to put your citation. A feature in your word processing program allows you to do this. In Microsoft Word and many other word processors, the footnote tool can be found under the references menu. The footnote will include a superscript number after the piece of information being cited.

No matter where the information is coming from, your in-text footnote will look the same as what you would put in a parenthetical. You will have a quote or paraphrase followed by a superscript number. The citation will go at the bottom of the page, with the number that matches the quote:

"There is no excuse for getting a citation wrong."[2]

Some professors prefer endnotes to footnotes. Endnotes are just like footnotes, except the citation goes at the end of the paper instead of the bottom of the page. Endnotes, like footnotes, can be inserted via the references tab in Microsoft Word.

The bibliography

In addition to inline citations, you will need to include a list of all of your sources in a bibliography or works cited page. As a general rule, each citation in your bibliography should include the author's name, the title of the source, the date when it was published and the publisher. You should alphabetize the list of sources in your bibliography.

 Tip #49

Consult a style guide to learn the exact citation formats for your bibliography.

Each citation style has slightly different rules for the bibliography, so make sure to look at online style guides. If you have questions about how to cite a particular source, ask a professor, a tutor, or a librarian for help.

---

2. Doe 2011, 15.

Check yourself

At the beginning of this chapter, you learned about the variety of actions that constitute plagiarism. The consequences of plagiarism might seem scary, but avoiding plagiarism is really quite easy. Always cite all of your sources. If you're not sure how to cite something, ask for help.

If you're worried about accidentally plagiarizing, the internet can actually help you out. Sites such as Write Check (**http://en.writecheck.com**) allow you to enter your paper and highlight any passages that seem similar to other writing, both on the internet and in many books.

Plagiarism doesn't happen by accident — as long as you are consciously trying to avoid plagiarism when writing your research paper, you will be fine.

 *Tip #50*

Even if it's late at night, you are confused about citations, and your paper is due in the morning, still try your best to cite your sources. It's better to try and possibly cite something incorrectly than to skip the citations and end up plagiarizing.

Chapter 6
The Body Of Your Paper

You've brainstormed about your topic, done your research, written your thesis, and organized your evidence — now there's nothing left to do except write your paper. It's time to open up a new document on the computer and begin typing.

 ## Tip #51

You don't have to write your paper in order.

Nearly all research papers follow the same basic structure. They begin with an introduction, continue with the body, and end with a conclusion. The final version of your paper must follow this formula, but you don't necessarily have to write your paper in this order. Some people find introductions to be one of the hardest parts of writing a paper. If you find yourself struggling to come up with a clever first line, skip it and move on. You might find that inspiration strikes while writing your paper's body paragraphs. This chapter will address how to write the body of your paper, while the next will address your introduction and conclusion.

The evidence you use in the body of your paper should come from the research you have already done. It's a good idea to keep your research notes and your notes from brainstorming close by when you are writing, that way, you don't forget important information.

Thinking About Writing

These days, most students write their papers on the computer. It makes sense — you don't have to worry about your handwriting and it's easy to make edits. However, it's also very easy to get distracted on the computer. Your mind wanders, so you go on the internet to check your favorite site for just a minute, but then you click on a video, and after it's done you click on another video . . . and an hour later you realize you haven't made any progress on your paper.

Tip #52

Avoid distractions while you are working on your paper. Find a place where you will not be interrupted. Put away your phone and stay off of websites that might suck up your time.

It's equally easy to get distracted by a cell phone or other electronic device. If you think your device might distract you, it's best to put it away completely — that way it can't interrupt your writing.

Tip #53

Make sure to save your paper as you begin writing and back up your file in multiple places. If something goes wrong with your computer, you don't want to lose all your work.

Computers seem like really great technology, but they're not perfect. Sometimes they catch viruses or fill up on memory space or crash unexpectedly. If you don't save your paper, you can lose your work. Make sure to save your files so that they can be accessed from more than one place—if you were writing and your computer unexpectedly shut down and never came back on, you should still be able to access your work.

A lot of students like to store their files on the internet, using programs such as Google Drive, iCloud, or Dropbox. You can also back up your paper to a USB drive or send new versions of the file via email—there are a lot of ways to save your work, just make sure to use one of them.

Tip #54

Writing is hard! It's OK to give yourself breaks. If you find your mind drifting, stand up, walk around, or get a drink of water.

If you haven't written a research paper before, you might be surprised to find that writing takes endurance. Don't try to write your whole paper in one sitting. Allow plenty of time and give yourself breaks, so you can refocus and do your best work. This also means you shouldn't leave your paper for the last minute. If you try to write it the night before, your options are pretty limited.

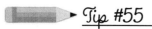 *Tip* #55

> Set a deadline for yourself to finish your paper that is before the actual
> due date. This way, you will have time to revise and edit.

You might think you're done once you've written the required number of pages. Writing a first draft of your paper is a good start, but it's important to revise and edit your paper afterwards. Techniques for revising and editing your paper will be found in Chapter 8.

Supporting Your Thesis

The entire purpose of the body of your paper is to support your thesis statement. Your thesis statement was just a statement. You told your reader what to believe. The rest of your paper is about showing your reader why you were right. Depending on your topic, there are many ways you can do this using quotes, logic, storytelling, statistics, or all of these and more.

Backing up your claims

When you've done your research well, you should have no trouble backing up your thesis. After all, you wrote your thesis based on your informed research. Still, even if you have a strong understanding of why your thesis is correct, it can still be hard to explain your arguments in a research paper.

> The way to make sure you are backing up your claims is by constantly asking yourself the important question: "Why is this true?"

For each point in your paper, ask yourself why that point is true. Then, write the specific details that support your point in relation to your thesis. Your research should provide these details — look at your notes. Each opinion you plan on presenting in your paper should have one, if not several, specific details to support it. Details matter because you must show readers why your point is valid rather than simply telling them they should believe what you are saying.

 *Tip #56*

Every fact in your paper should work toward supporting your thesis.

For example, say you're writing a paper about climate change. Your thesis is that governments should limit carbon emissions to help slow the rate of climate change. Your first claim is that humans have caused the planet to get warmer. Why is this true? You can cite scientific data about the warming of the planet. You can explain scientific processes, such as the greenhouse effect, that seem to be causing this warming. You could quote well-renowned scientists saying that climate change is a real problem. These quotes, data, and logic are your evidence. They work together to support your claim that climate change is human-caused, which helps support your thesis.

> When you are incorporating details from your notes into your paper, don't forget to include citations! If you are unsure how to cite something, indicate to yourself somehow (for example, by using a brightly-colored font) that you must still insert a citation. This way, you don't forget to cite something and accidentally plagiarize. If you need a refresher on citations or avoiding plagiarism, look back to Chapter 5.

Structuring Your Paper

Organization is essential to any good research paper. You must present your ideas in a way that your reader can easily follow and understand. This next section will address the various strategies you can use to structure your paper, and the situations where each one might work best.

Often, the best way to determine the structure of your paper is to first write an outline. An outline can help you determine the order of your ideas and their relation to one another. For more on how to make an outline, refer back to Chapter 2.

 **Tip #57**

> If you find you are confused or are writing the same thing over and over again, go back and look at your research or your outline. Don't waste your time writing when you don't know what you want to say.

How to organize your ideas

Sometimes your professor might have a very specific idea for how they'd like you to structure your paper. Many scientific papers, for example, follow a standard structure. Make sure to read your assignment and rubric carefully to see if your professor requires a certain structure.

The purpose of structure is to make sure your reader doesn't get confused. You can test your paper for structure by reading it through and asking yourself whether there are places where a reader wouldn't have enough information. If the answer is yes, you probably need to add more information or change the order of ideas in your paper.

Chronological

If your paper involves telling a story or explaining events, it probably is a good idea to make it chronological—telling things in the order that they happened. Most history papers should be structured chronologically, as they typically involve events that happened in some succession. A chronologically organized paper is also a good way to showcase cause and effect. If you are trying to prove that one thing caused another, it's important to give your reader a clear idea of the timing.

If you are planning on writing your paper chronologically, you might try writing a timeline or bullet points with key events as part of your brainstorming. You can use this timeline as a template when you begin writing your actual paper.

Comparing different ideas

Some research papers may ask you to compare different ideas and come to a conclusion. The structure of your paper can reflect these comparisons. For example, if you are asked to analyze two different novels for a paper, you might divide the body of your paper into three sections, analyzing the first novel, the second novel, and the similarities or differences between them.

Structuring your paper around comparison also works well if you are asked to analyze cause-and-effect. For example, if you were writing a paper about the factors that led to the 2008 recession, you could pick three factors based on your research that led to the recession. In your paper, you would analyze each of these factors individually, and then conclude the body of your paper with a discussion about which factors were most impactful and how each related to the other ones.

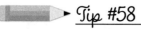 *Tip #58*

If your paper is very long, you can break it down into sections or mini-chapters.

Developing theories

College-level research papers sometimes ask students to analyze or apply a particularly theory or philosophy. For example, a literature class might ask you to consider how nihilism applies in Dostoevsky's *Crime and Punishment*. For a sociology class, you might analyze how Freud's understanding of human sexuality applies to online dating today.

Most readers aren't terribly familiar with nihilism or Freudian theories of sexuality. If you're writing a paper that involves one of these, you probably want to provide a brief overview of the philosophy at the beginning of your paper. Your reader will understand your thesis better if they understand the theories that it is based on.

(Maybe) not just words

Depending on the subject of your paper, you might consider incorporating visuals into your paper. For example, if you are writing about science, graphs or tables showcasing scientific results might be useful. If your paper is about art history, you might want to include renderings of the art that you are writing about. Check with your professor — they may have very specific ideas on how or if you should include these visual aids.

▸ Tip #59

Depending on your topic and subject area, you may choose to include pictures, charts, graphs, or other visuals in your paper. Unless your instructor tells you otherwise, these visuals should be labeled with a caption and should be referenced directly in your text.

If you want to include visuals with your research paper, you need to make sure they are genuinely relevant. Don't just include a picture or a graph because you think it's cool — it must directly support your thesis. To ensure your visuals are relevant for your reader, you should reference them in the text. The next two examples show how you can do this.

Average global temperatures have increased steadily over the last 50 years. (See Graph 1).

The "big-eyes" style that Keane used in her paintings was unlike anything American art had seen before. (See Photograph 1).

Graph 1 would be a plot of average global temperatures over the last 50 years; Photograph 1 would be a picture of one of Margaret Keane's paintings. In both of these cases, the visuals would help the reader to better understand the writer's point.

 **Tip #60**

If you didn't create your visuals yourself, don't forget to cite them!

Research Paper Style

The structure of your paper helps to make sure that your ideas are easy to follow. The other essential component to making your work readable is writing style. The remainder of this chapter will consider how to write sentences that sound good, weave those sentences into paragraphs, and incorporate quotes and evidence.

> The tone of your paper refers to your attitude toward your reader, which you show through your word choices. For example, the tone of this book is fairly informal. The book directly addresses you, the reader. It uses contractions and sometimes exclamation points.

Tip #61

Avoid using contractions when writing a research paper.

The tone of your research paper should generally be formal. Contractions are considered informal, because they mimic how people speak, so you should avoid them in your paper. You should also avoid exclamation points, as well as words like "I," "you," and "we." Research papers are focused on ideas — using the first or second person emphasizes yourself or your reader, whereas you want the focus to be on your arguments and evidence.

Tip #62

Avoid using the first person ("I") and the second person ("you") when writing a research paper.

Types of sentences

You probably think you know a lot about sentences. You've definitely written sentences before—which makes writing your paper much easier. After all, research papers are made up of many sentences. While anyone can write many sentences, not all sentences are created equally. This section will go over the various kinds of sentences, and how to use each of them effectively in your paper.

Basic sentence structure

Sentences are made up of clauses. Each clause must have at least one subject and verb. There are four basic types of sentences. The most basic is the simple sentence, which has just one clause. The following two sentences are examples of simple sentences.

> Dostoyevsky wrote *Crime and Punishment* in 1866.
>
> The British and German soldiers played soccer and took pictures together.

Note that the second example is still a simple sentence, despite using the word "and" twice. The British and German soldiers are together a singular subject. The clause has two verbs—"played" and "took"—however, since both of these verbs reference the same subject, they are still part of the same clause.

A compound sentence is made up of two or more clauses, connected by a coordinating conjunction. The clauses in a compound sentence must be independent, meaning that they could each stand on their own. You can remember the seven coordinating conjunctions using the acronym FANBOYS: for, and, no, but, or, yet and so.

The following are a few examples of compound sentences.

> The wise student backed up his work in several places, for he knew his computer might crash at any moment.
>
> The British soldiers played soccer and the German soldiers took pictures.

Note how this last example differs from the one in the previous section. This time, there are two clauses — "The British soldiers played soccer" and "the German soldiers took pictures." Each of these clauses could be their own simple sentence. When connected by a coordinating conjunction, they form a compound sentence.

 *Tip #63*

Don't start sentences with coordinating conjunctions.

When people talk, they often start sentences with coordinating conjunctions. For example, if you learn you have three exams on the same day, you might respond, "But that's not fair!" Since a research paper is more formal than these everyday conversations, avoid using coordinating conjunctions at the beginning of sentences when you are writing.

Complex sentences are made up of multiple clauses, like compound sentences. However, complex sentences are typically composed of one independent clause and one dependent clause. A dependent clause begins with a subordinating conjunction. It cannot stand on its own as a sentence. The following are examples of complex sentences, with the subordinating conjunction underlined.

> <u>Although</u> the general knew about the dangers, he still decided to attack.

The English and German soldiers spent time together, <u>even though</u> they both knew they would have to fight against each other the next day.

Complex-compound sentences typically have three clauses, connected by both a coordinating and subordinating conjunction. Take a look at the following examples and identify the conjunctions in each.

Although the general knew about the dangers, he still decided to attack and many men were killed.

After the flood washed away the cornfields, some of the farmers tried to rebuild and others decided to leave for the city.

Tip #64

Use a mix of simple, complex, compound, and complex-compound sentences.

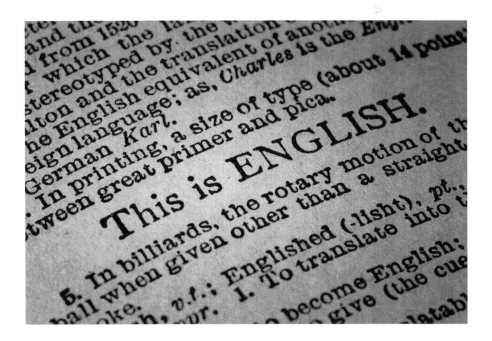

In your writing, you want to use a mix of sentence types. If you rely only on simple sentences, your writing will sound harsh and choppy. On the other hand, if all of your sentences are complex and compound, your writing may be very difficult to follow. It is important to strike a balance with sentence types in your paper.

Things to avoid

A rhetorical question is a question that someone asks without expecting an answer. Any question you ask in your paper will be rhetorical, because you aren't actually there to have a conversation with your reader.

 *Tip #65*

Don't use rhetorical questions in the body of your research paper.

Rhetorical questions can occasionally be effective in introductions or conclusions, but they don't work as well in the body of your paper. You should be presenting evidence to back up your thesis—not asking your reader questions. The following example showcases a passage that uses a rhetorical question, and shows how to create the same effect without using a question.

> Readers of *Crime and Punishment* are left wondering: did Raskolnikov really have to kill Lizaveta? Although the circumstances of the novel indicate that her death was unnecessary, her murder is in fact essential to Raskolnikov's symbolic redemption at the end of the novel.

> When Raskolnikov kills Lizaveta during the botched robbery, her death seems highly unnecessary. However, as the novel progresses, her death becomes a driving force that leads Raskolnikov to confess and ultimately find redemption.

 *Tip #66*

Try to avoid passive voice in your writing, unless you are writing about science.

Passive voice, and its counterpart active voice, refer to who or what in a sentence is completing the action described by the verb. When a sentence is in active voice, the subject of the sentence completes the action described by the verb. When a sentence is in passive voice, the verb acts upon the subject of the sentence, and the person or thing that completes the action is described in a prepositional phrase, or left out entirely. If that sounds confusing, it's much easier to see active and passive voice through examples. Take a look below.

Passive voice: The ball was thrown by Bob.
Active voice: Bob threw the ball.

Passive voice: The bomb was dropped.
Active voice: The plane dropped the bomb.

Many times, the passive voice sounds awkward and makes your sentences wordier. More importantly, the passive voice de-emphasizes the person who completes the action, which can be confusing. In fact, writers sometimes intentionally use passive voice when they are trying not to reveal information—but you shouldn't do this in your research paper!

The following are a few examples of passive voice that could come up in your writing, and how you can fix it.

Passive voice: Raskolnikov was followed around the city by the detective Porfiry Petrovich.

Active voice: The detective Porfiry Petrovich followed Raskolnikov around the city.

Passive voice: Studies found that the children were helped by their time in preschool.
Active voice: Studies found that time in preschool benefited the children.

While you should usually try to avoid passive voice, many professors in science classes prefer that you use passive voice, particularly when you are describing scientific experiments or methods. Always follow your professors' preferences when you are writing your paper!

From sentences to paragraphs

You've probably been writing paragraphs for a long time. The body of your research paper is really just a series of well-written paragraphs. A strong paragraph in a research paper has four key elements: a topic sentence, a coherent progression, supporting details, and an ending transition.

The topic sentence is the first sentence of your paragraph. It should give the reader a general idea of what the paragraph will discuss. The rest of the sentences in your paragraph should in some way relate to your topic sentence.

A good paragraph should have at least three supporting details. Some paragraphs may have more than this, but three is a good number to aim for. If you cannot come up with three supporting details, then you will either need to do more research or adjust the topic of your paragraph.

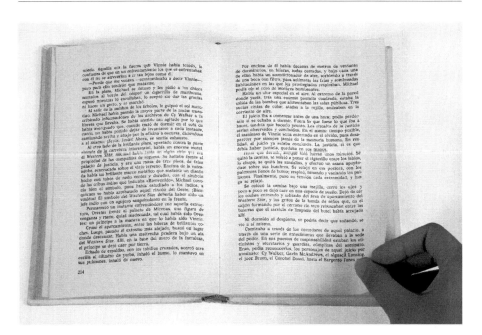

It's important that your paragraph flows cleanly between these supporting details. Ask yourself: what is the most logical order for presenting my ideas? Sometimes, certain ideas may rely on one another.

► *Tip #67*

As a general rule, stick to one idea per paragraph. Obviously, your sentences will provide more details on your topic, but if you find yourself talking about a new idea, you should also be starting a new paragraph.

A common mistake that college students make is writing long, winding paragraphs that stray from the main idea. When you get to the end of a paragraph, ask yourself: Am I still writing about the topic from the beginning of the paragraph? If the answer is no, considering splitting up your writing into multiple paragraphs.

Regardless of how you choose to structure your paper, it is important to use transitions to indicate to your reader when you are moving between ideas.

Include transitions between every paragraph so that your paper flows neatly.

 *Tip #68*

Use transitions to guide your reader — don't just skip from one idea to the next.

Some transitions (such as "additionally" or "likewise") indicate that you will be staying with the same idea. Others (such as "by contrast" or "on the other hand") indicate that you will be bringing up a different idea. Transitions can also describe a different time or place. Take a look at the following list of transition words, and see if you can think of any to add.

• Additionally	• As well as	• After
• Likewise	• Therefore	• Following
• In addition	• Unlike	• Ultimately
• Similarly	• By contrast	• Finally
• Furthermore	• On the other hand	
• Moreover	• However	

Transition words are not the only way to move between ideas in your paper. While transition words are useful, your paper may begin to sound repetitive if you use them in every paragraph. You can also transition between ideas by repeating important words or phrases, or by using chronology or cause-and-effect to make your ideas clear. The next two examples show a transition between two paragraphs — with and without transition words.

Example with a transition word: The proximity between the United States and Mexico made it easy for immigrant workers to come to the United States only temporarily. Mexican immigration records from 1911 and 1912 show that the number of Mexicans who immigrated to the United States in those years was roughly the same as the number who returned to Mexico.

However, the Mexican Revolution led to a decline in the reciprocity of immigration between the United States and Mexico. The conflict, especially following the assassination of President Francisco Madero in 1913, resulted in an influx of migrants and refugees from Mexico to the United States.

Example without a transition word: The proximity between the United States and Mexico made it easy for immigrant workers to come to the United States only temporarily. Mexican immigration records from 1911 and 1912 show that the number of Mexicans who immigrated to the United States in those years was roughly the same as the number who returned to Mexico—a reciprocal pattern of immigration.

Reciprocity resulting from temporary immigration declined as a result of the Mexican Revolution. The conflict, especially following the assassination of President Francisco Madero in 1913, resulted in an influx of migrants from Mexico to the United States.

This second example works well because the first sentence of the second paragraph uses two words "reciprocity" and "temporary" which clearly tie it to the previous paragraph. Furthermore, the end of the previous paragraph mentions the years 1911 and 1912, while the new paragraph mentions the year 1913—making the progression seem logical. No transition word is necessary.

Incorporating quotes

Quotes are an essential form of evidence for nearly any research paper. Chapter 5 discussed how to properly cite quotes; this section will address how to incorporate them into the body of your paper. There are several different ways you can integrate a quote into your writing—which one you will use depends on the length of the quote and the context.

Tip #69

If you are only quoting a few words or a phrase, you can incorporate the quote directly into your writing.

If you only want to quote a few words from another author, it's fairly easy to incorporate their work into your writing. Look at the following example.

> Raskolnikov shows his distaste for Alyona Ivanovna, describing her as an "old crone," (9).

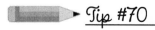

Tip #70

If your quote is at least a sentence long, it should stand alone grammatically in your writing.

Often, you will want to quote more than just a few words. If you are quoting a full clause or sentence, the quote should be able to stand alone in your writing. In these cases, you introduce your quote with a colon, as in the following examples.

> When Sonya gives Raskolnikov the cross, she symbolically links her suffering and his: "Sonya silently took two crosses from a drawer, one of cypress, the other of brass; she crossed herself, crossed him, and hung the cypress cross around his neck," (522).

> Access to preschool has become a key issue, in particular because of the growing number of children who live in households where both parents work: "The structure of U.S. society has been rapidly

changing during the past three decades due to the increasing movement of women into the paid labor force, now estimated to include over half of all women with children under age 6," (Peisner-Feinberg and Burchinal, 1997, pg. 451).

 *Tip #71*

If you are using a quote that is four lines or longer, you must format it as a block quote.

Quotes that are very long are known as block quotes, and must be formatted differently. Like a regular quote, a block quote should be able to stand on its own grammatically, and should be introduced with a colon. Block quotes are set on their own lines and are indented. They do not use quotation marks. Look at the following example.

Dostoyevsky paints Raskolnikov's childhood as dark, and these early struggles clearly still haunt him years later:

> Raskolnikov had a terrible dream. He dreamed of his childhood, while still in their little town. He is about seven years old and is strolling with his father on a feast day, towards evening, outside of town. The weather is gray, the day is stifling, the countryside is exactly as it was preserved in his memory: it was even far more effaced in his memory than it appeared now in his dream. The town stands open to view; there is not a single willow tree around it; somewhere very far off, at the very edge of the sky, is the black line of a little forest. (54)

Generally, you must use a block quote if you are quoting a passage that is four lines or longer. You should use block quotes sparingly—the purpose of your research paper is to develop your ideas and support them with evidence. If you spend too much of your paper on long quotes, you won't have much space for your own ideas.

Tip #72

When you include a quote, you probably will need to explain it. Don't let your explanation of your quote begin with "This quote shows . . ." or a similar phrase.

Quotes are essential pieces of evidence that support your thesis, but your paper should not be simply a series of quotes. You also need to explain to your reader how each quote is relevant and supports your thesis. As a general rule, every quote that you use in your research paper should be followed by an explanation that is at least as long as the quote.

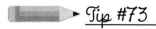

Tip #73

Remember, a quote means you are taking the words and ideas of someone else. If you are using a quote in your research paper, you should always have a citation to go along with it.

Quotes require you to use inline citations in your paper. Always put an inline citation at the end of a sentence, regardless of the piece of information that the citation refers to. If you need a refresher on using inline citations, refer to Chapter 5.

Keep in mind

It might seem like you have a lot to worry about in the body of your paper—quotes, visuals, citations, and transitions. Rather than thinking of these elements as requirements you have to meet, think of them as tools you have at your disposal. You have done a lot of research; the body of your paper is about finding the best way to communicate everything you have learned.

If you get confused, look at your notes or your thesis to get yourself back on track. Otherwise, take a deep breath and write down the things you know. You're going to be fine!

 *Tip #74*

Recognize the importance of your own writing style. Don't pretend to be a stuffy academic or write like you think someone else would write. It's your paper. Let your voice shine through.

Chapter 7
Introductions And Conclusions

Your introduction and conclusion make up only a small proportion of your paper. In shorter research papers, your introduction and conclusion may each be only a paragraph. Even in very long papers, the introduction and conclusion will likely take up only a few pages each.

Although your introduction and conclusion are short, they are not something you can slack on. The introduction sets the tone for your paper, while the conclusion is the last thing your reader remembers. This chapter will address how to write introductions and conclusions to make sure your paper begins and ends strong.

Your Intro

Your introduction is the first impression readers get of your paper. If they do not like it, they will not want to keep reading. Your professor will hopefully read the entire paper anyway, but you would like your professor to be impressed by the start of your paper, rather than disappointed.

Some students think that their introduction must be flashy or shocking to catch their readers' attention. You definitely want your introduction to be interesting, but you can pique your readers' interest in many different ways. Generally, you want to use your introduction to show your reader why your topic is significant or relevant. You might connect your paper to a broader subject that everyone knows about. For example, if you are writing about the novel *Crime and Punishment*, you might explain how the theme of cultural conflict is relevant both in the novel and in our modern world. If you are writing about preschool and child development, you can tell your reader that this research has real policy implications which could impact children in the United States.

Your introduction should also provide a roadmap for the rest of your paper. For example, if your paper is comparing two novels, your introduction should name both novels and tell your reader what about them you will be comparing. If your paper is analyzing the factors that led to a particular historical event, you should tell your reader the event and the factors you will discuss.

Finally, your introduction should include your thesis statement. Typically, the thesis statement will go at the end of your introduction, allowing you to introduce your topic before you arrive at your thesis.

> An inverted pyramid, or upside-down triangle, is a good rule to follow when writing your introduction. Just as an inverted pyramid is widest at the top and then narrows to a point, your introduction should start out broad and then narrow down to your specific topic and thesis statement.

Your hook

The hook is the first sentence — or first few sentences — of your introduction. The best way to find a hook is to compose a sentence that is interesting and segues nicely into your argument. This will allow you reel the reader in and then direct their attention to the main point of your paper.

Tip #75

Begin your paper with a hook — a sentence that is intriguing or exciting and makes your reader want to learn more.

There is no single formula for writing a good hook. Some writers like to use shocking facts or statistics to open their paper. If your hook is surprising, your reader will want to keep reading to learn more. Below are a few examples of introductions that use shocking facts as hooks:

According to statistics from the Bureau of Justice, over 100 million Americans have some sort of criminal record.[3] That is about one-third of the country's population. The large number of Americans with criminal records can largely be attributed to the War on Drugs, which began in the 1970s. The War on Drugs also led the

---

3. "Americans with Criminal Records," *The Sentencing Project*. 2015. Web.

United States to lock up more criminals, leading to a massive growth in the prison population. However, many people who are in prison are not dangerous criminals, and keeping them locked up is expensive for taxpayers. Therefore, the United States should consider policies that reduce the number of people in prison.

What works: Many people are surprised to learn that 100 million Americans have criminal records. This fact draws in your reader. This introduction then transitions well to the topic of the paper — why the United States should imprison less people.

The Bubonic Plague — which swept through Europe and Asia in the fourteenth century — may have killed over one-third of the world population.[4] Better sanitary practices and the innovation of antibiotics have helped prevent another plague like that from happening again. However, the growth of antibiotic-resistant bacteria poses a serious public health threat and raises the specter that another disease as bad as the Bubonic Plague could strike again.

What works: A plague that killed one-third of people in the world is pretty shocking! Although this paper isn't about the Bubonic Plague — it's about antibiotic resistance — this introduction works especially well because the author uses the plague as a point of comparison, rather than just a "fun" fact.

Anecdotes, or short relevant stories, can also be good hooks. Some anecdotes are entertaining, while others can make a key point about your paper. Just make sure if you use an anecdote that it is relevant to your topic. Some

---

4. M. J. Keeling and C. A. Gilligan, "Bubonic Plague: A Metapopulation Model of a Zoonosis." *Proceedings: Biological Sciences* 267, no. 1458 (2000): 2219.

students are tempted to use any funny or clever story, but if your anecdote is not relevant, it might confuse your reader.

> Bad anecdotal introduction: When John Adams was at the Constitutional Convention, his wife Abigail sent him letters telling him not to forget about women's rights too. However, the movement for women's rights in the United States did not really gain steam until Susan B. Anthony became a leader in the 1800s. Although Anthony did not live long enough to see women gain the right to vote in 1920, her contributions to the women's suffrage movement were invaluable, and she should be remembered as one of the most impactful women in American history.

What's wrong: The anecdote in this opening attempts to tell the story of Abigail Adams telling her husband to "remember the ladies" in the Constitution — something he and the rest of its writers failed to do. However, this anecdote is confusing for a paper about Susan B. Anthony. Although Anthony's efforts ultimately led to more constitutional rights for women, this anecdote introduces too many people and makes the introduction confusing.

> Good anecdotal introduction: In 1872, a woman was arrested in Rochester, New York. Her crime? She had tried to vote at a time when women in the United States were not granted voting rights. The woman, named Susan B. Anthony, was one of the most prominent advocates for women's voting rights in the 20th century. Although she did not live long enough to see women gain the right to vote in 1920, her contributions to the women's suffrage movement were invaluable, and she should be remembered as one of the most impactful women in American history.

What works: The anecdote is interesting. A reader who reads the first sentence will be intrigued — who is this women? Why was she arrested? Unlike the previous example, however, this anecdote is focused and highly relevant to the writer's thesis, creating a smooth transition.

The best anecdotes are vivid and specific. Consider starting your paper with a detailed description of a person, place, or scene that is central to your topic. Readers will immediately be drawn in by your details.

Things to avoid

You're not the first person to write a research paper introduction. Some introduction strategies have been used so frequently that they become cliché. You want to make your introduction sound original, so don't repeat these commonly-used techniques.

 **Tip #76**

Avoid clichés in your introduction.

Questions are a common introduction cliché. If you want to use a question to lead into your introduction, try starting with a statement that leads into the question and then asking the question a few sentences into the introduction. Below are a few examples of question introductions, and how to revise them.

Original hook: Would you know how to feed your family if you made less than $2 each day? According to the World Bank, 767 million people in the world make less than $1.90 per day.[5]

What to do: In this case, the introduction includes a very compelling statistic. Skip the question and begin with the statistic.

Revised hook: Nearly 11 percent of the world's population, 767 million people, make less than $1.90 per day, according to World Bank statistics.

Original hook: What if the technology your phone uses could also help reduce gun deaths? Several technology people have created

---

5. World Bank. 2016. *Poverty and Shared Prosperity 2016: Taking on Inequality.* Washington, DC: World Bank. Web.

something called a smart gun — a weapon that uses fingerprint technology to prevent accidental shootings.[6]

What to do: The question used in this introduction could easily be rewritten as a statement.

Revised hook: Technology developers believe that technology similar to what an iPhone uses could also help reduce gun deaths. They have created something called a smart gun — a weapon that uses fingerprint technology to prevent accidental shootings.

Quotations are another common introduction cliché. Some students try to begin their introductions with famous quotations that may have little to do with their research subjects. Here are a few examples of bad quotation use in an introduction.

"Ask not what your country can do for you; ask what you can do for your country," said President John F. Kennedy in his inaugural address in 1960.[7] In fact, Kennedy's assertion in 1960 could easily be applied to Americans today as the country struggles to address climate change.

What's wrong: The research paper is about climate change. Quoting President Kennedy might make the author sound smart, but it's actually irrelevant to the paper.

"To be, or not to be, that is the question," wrote William Shakespeare in his famous play, *Hamlet.* Although this is the most well-known quote from *Hamlet,* Shakespeare's play is actually about much more than just this one line.

---

6. Nicholas Kristof, "Smart Guns Save Lives. So Where Are They?" *New York Times,* 17 Jan 2015, Web.
7. Ralph Keyes, "Ask Not Where This Quote Came From," *Washington Post,* 4 June 2006, Web.

What's wrong: The assertion that *Hamlet* is about more than "to be, or not to be" isn't surprising — any play will be about more than just one line. Furthermore, since everyone knows this line, it doesn't serve as a particularly intriguing hook.

Occasionally, it makes sense to use quotations in your introduction, if the quotation is especially powerful and specific to your topic. The following is an example of an introduction that uses a quotation but avoids being too cliché.

"Suddenly there was an enormous flash of light, the brightest light I have ever seen or I think anyone has ever seen . . . there was an enormous ball of fire which grew and grew and rolled as it grew; it went up into the air, and yellow flashed into scarlet and green. It looked menacing."[8] This menacing ball of light described by scientist Isidor Rabi was the test of the first atomic bomb on July 16, 1945. Although Rabi could see the pure physical power of the bomb, he had no idea about the geopolitical implications it would soon bring to the world.

What works: This quote is very vivid, so it will help draw in your reader. Since it's not well-known, your reader doesn't yet know what to expect, which makes it less cliché. The sentence after the quote helps pivot from the hook to the subject of the paper: the political consequences of the atomic bomb.

Metaphors or analogies are another way some students like to start their research papers. If your metaphor or analogy is original and specific to your topic, it can make a very effective introduction. However, metaphors and analogies can often become overused.

---

8. Edward T. Sullivan, *The Ultimate Weapon: The Race to Develop the Atomic Bomb,* (New York: Holiday House, 2007), 5.

How do you tell if a metaphor has become a cliché? Ask yourself if the metaphor actually invokes a strong image or feeling in your head. If it does, then it's fine. But if you immediately know what the metaphor means so that it doesn't give you any special image or new sense of meaning, it's probably a cliché.

For example, take the phrase "beating a dead horse," which refers to doing something useless or unhelpful again and again. This metaphor is used so frequently that it has become a cliché — when someone says this, people don't envision someone beating a dead horse. They just immediately assume the meaning.

If you are unsure whether your metaphor is cliché, ask around to see if other people have heard something similar before. Alternately, type phrases into a search engine and see what comes back. If a lot of people have used the same metaphor on the internet, it's probably a cliché.

Transitioning to your thesis

A hook isn't the only important part of an introduction. As you've probably noticed in the examples, the sentences that come after the hook help draw a connection between your hook and the point of your paper.

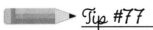 ► *Tip #77*

Your introduction should end with your thesis statement.

You probably remember thesis statements from Chapter 2. The thesis statement tells the main point of your paper—you should have written it before you started writing the rest of your paper. Typically, your thesis statement will go at the end of your introduction. If you are following the inverted pyramid method, your thesis statement is the narrow part.

What goes between your hook and your thesis statement? Depending on the topic of your paper, you might just use a few quick transition sentences. You might also use the introduction to provide context about your topic. For example, if you are writing about the novel *Crime and Punishment*, you might use your introduction to provide some basic historic context, as shown in the next example.

In the 19th century, Europe experienced several transformations. Rapid industrialization changed the nature of the economy and spurred massive population growth in major cities. Technology also enabled the rapid spread of new philosophical ideas across the continent. However, not everyone was happy with these changes. The novel *Crime and Punishment* by Fyodor Dostoyevsky uses religious references to emphasize the importance of traditional Russian values. The novel can be viewed as a pushback again the encroachment of Western ideals into Russia during the 19th century.

This thesis argues that the novel *Crime and Punishment* fights back against Western ideals. This introduction provides context by giving the reader a basic understanding of where these ideas are coming from. The hook in this introduction is very broad, but it quickly narrows to the writer's thesis.

If unsure about how to tackle your introduction, remember the three basic parts: hook, transition, and thesis statement. If you're unsure of how to come up with a hook, think about something in your research that you found interesting or funny or strange. Chances are, your readers will feel the same way.

Your Conclusion

If you've arrived at the conclusion, your paper is probably almost done. Although you might be excited to finish, don't rush while writing your conclusion. The conclusion determines what a reader will remember from a paper — it's your job to make sure your reader takes away the right message.

Earlier in this chapter, we discussed the inverted pyramid method for introductions — starting out broad and narrowing to the thesis. Conclusions are the opposite. Your conclusion should be structured like a pyramid. You should begin by restating the main point of your paper, and then expand to something broader.

Restating your thesis

 ► *Tip #78*

Your conclusion should restate your thesis in different words.

One key component of the conclusion is the restatement of the thesis. Your restated thesis should address the same points as your original thesis, but should seem final, rather than introductory. This time, you are not telling the reader what you are going to attempt to prove; you are telling them what you have already proven in your paper.

Many students struggle to restate their thesis using different words. After all, they carefully picked the wording of their thesis statement the first time. The next example takes a sample thesis statement from Chapter 2 and shows how a writer might restate it in a conclusion.

Original thesis statement: Research has repeatedly shown that children who attend preschool get better grades and are more likely to graduate high school than their counterparts. Therefore, providing universal access to preschool should be a priority for education policymakers.

Restated thesis statement: When examining recent research in early childhood development, it is clear that preschool attendance vastly improves future academic outcomes for children. Policymakers should look to universal access to preschool as a key component in improving public education.

Why this works: This restatement provides the same information as the original thesis. The phrase "when examining recent research" reminds the reader of the evidence that the writer presumably presented in the paper, which makes the restatement effective for a conclusion.

Going over key points

Research papers are usually very long! Just as the introduction provided a roadmap of what the paper would discuss, the conclusion should remind your reader of what they have just read. If you're not sure what the key points of your paper are, take a look at your topic sentences — they should recap the important concepts.

You want to summarize the key points of your paper in your conclusion without going into too much detail. You can repeat particularly striking quotations or statistics, but try not to use more than one or two. The conclusion represents your closing thoughts on the topic, so it should primarily consist of your own words.

> While summary is important, it isn't enough for your conclusion. Summarization is necessary to remind the reader of what the main points are, but it does not tell readers what they should learn and take away from your paper. Try to keep summarization to no more than half of your conclusion.

New ideas

 Tip #79

Don't introduce major new ideas in your conclusion.

This tip might seem to counter what you've learned; after all, the pyramid structure says that you are supposed to broaden from your thesis. The trick is to do both: you should expand from your thesis, but without broaching a completely new subject. For example, if your research paper has been analyzing a novel, you might address in your conclusion how the lessons from the novel apply in the real world. You wouldn't bring up other novels from the same author and suggest that your reader check them out.

Sometimes students bring up new ideas in their conclusions because they think of new points while they are writing the conclusion. If this happens to you, go back and add these ideas to the body of your paper.

Avoiding loose ends

Loose ends refer to unresolved questions your reader might have about your paper. You want to avoid loose ends as much as possible. While it is OK for your reader to be thinking about the implications of your paper afterwards, your reader shouldn't be left hanging because you didn't include enough information.

For example, if you have written a paper exposing a major social problem, your reader might be left wondering what they can do to take action. That's an important idea. However, if your reader finished the paper and still doesn't understand how the social problem was caused, that is a loose end. Go back and add information to your paper.

Making it memorable

A good research paper will educate its reader about a topic. A great research paper will leave the reader thinking for days afterwards, inspired to learn more. While a conclusion won't make or break your paper, a strong conclusion will help make your paper memorable.

 *Tip #80*

Your conclusion should make it clear to your reader why they should care about what they just read.

Many research paper topics are abstract or seemingly unrelated to everyday life. A conclusion should show your reader how to apply the lessons from your paper or suggest how other researchers could explore the topic in the future. For example, if you've been analyzing a novel, ask yourself how the lessons from the novel might apply to your readers' life. If you've written a paper in the sciences, you might suggest how future research could provide more insight on the topic.

Clever conclusion techniques

 *Tip #81*

> Create a connection between your introduction and your conclusion.
> For example, if you used a clever hook in your introduction, see if you
> can tie the same words or concept into your conclusion.

Drawing a connection between your introduction and conclusion is one way to make your paper memorable for your reader. The following examples take a couple of the sample introduction hooks from earlier in the chapter and show how the same ideas could be used in a conclusion.

Introduction hook: According to statistics from the Bureau of Justice, over 100 million Americans have some sort of criminal record.

Concluding sentence: Criminal justice reform is not easy, but given that over 100 million Americans have a criminal record, it is necessary.

Introduction hook: The Bubonic Plague—which swept through Europe and Asia in the fourteenth century—may have killed over one-third of the world population.

Concluding sentence: Governments should take the problem of antibiotic resistance seriously — after all, nobody wants another Bubonic Plague.

✏ *Tip #82*

End your conclusion with a memorable line.

> If you think of your paper as a meal, the final line of your conclusion is like the last bite your reader takes—the flavor will linger in his or her mouth for a long time after. You want to make this last bite as tasty as possible.

To make your last line strong, you should watch out for a few key characteristics. First, your last line should be definitive — don't use words like "maybe" or "perhaps" or "possibly," all of which indicate that you are uncertain. Your last line should also be broad. A broad last line fits with the pyramid strategy, and makes your reader connect your paper to the outside world.

Putting it all together

The following is a sample conclusion from a paper about the novel *Crime and Punishment*. To remind yourself what the paper was about, take a look at the outline for this paper, which was in Chapter 2. Although you haven't read the paper that would go along with this conclusion, see if you can identify which part of the conclusion restates the thesis, which parts summarize the key points of the paper, and which parts tell the reader what message to take away.

> The conflict between Western and Russian values is evident in Fyodor Dostoyevsky's 19th century novel *Crime and Punishment*. Raskolnikov's theories — which reflect radical European philosophies — make him a murderer and leave him wracked with guilt, and he only finds salvation after he embraces religion. His confession and prison sentence represent his attempt to pay for his sins,

and his ultimate atonement at the end of the novel validates the traditional Russian order. Raskolnikov learns the hard way that no man is above the law, and that morals still apply even in a rapidly changing world. His lessons reflect broader conflicts over progress and industrialization, which not only played out in Russia in the 19th century, but also continue to occur in the world today.

There you have it. Once you have written your conclusion, you are finished with the first draft of your paper. Congratulate yourself, but don't print out it out and turn it in quite yet. The remaining chapters will discuss how to revise, edit, and format your paper so that your final version is even better than your first.

Chapter 8
Editing And Revising

Writing a research paper is a bit like racing through a giant maze. When you are in the maze, you can only make small decisions — do you go right or left? Sometimes, you run into dead ends and have to turn around. These mistakes are part of the process: if you stand in place, afraid to make errors, you will never get out of the maze. If you refuse to write because your sentences aren't perfect, you'll never finish your paper. When you finish your first draft, it's like you have completed the maze for the first time. Even though you've finished your task, you probably didn't do it perfectly. Once you are on the outside, you can look at the maze from above. You see the big picture; you notice your mistakes and you have the chance to correct them. You might notice that there's a much easier path than you saw your first time through.

Making changes to the first draft of your paper is known as revising and editing. This part of the process is often neglected; many college students don't finish a paper until the night before it is due, which leaves no time for revising. Other students will use spell-check as their only form of editing, even if they have time to be more thorough. If you are the kind of student who typically skips revising and editing, now is the time to break that habit.

Time is essential when it comes to revising and editing. Some students find it helpful to pretend their papers are due a day sooner than they really are, which creates extra time to revise and edit. If you have time, it's a good idea to take a break before you start editing your paper. If you are able to get a good night's sleep, or even just work on something for a different class, you will be able to look at your paper with a fresh set of eyes, which will make you more likely to notice your errors.

 *Tip #83*

Ask a friend to read your paper for you. Listen to their suggestions and decide what changes you would like to make.

It can be difficult to be objective about your own paper for several reasons. First, your familiarity with your paper inhibits your ability to edit. Since you have read your own words so many times, you will miss errors because you subconsciously change what a sentence actually says to what it should say.

Furthermore, you probably wrote your paper in a way that makes sense to you. However, you are not the audience for your own paper. When you have written a research paper, you are likely close to an expert on the topic, which means you might not realize if you have failed to provide enough context or if your ideas seem out of order. It is risky to assume that a reader will be able to follow your logic and argument, even when you have done excellent research. Editing and revising are about ensuring your paper makes sense to other people, too. Asking for other people's opinions can help you figure this out.

While it is a good idea to seek input from others, your paper still belongs to you. As the writer, you have final say in what changes you make. You don't have to follow advice from others, but you should be open to it. Some writers are so proud of their work—or so reluctant to make changes—that they refuse to listen to advice from others. Don't be stubborn or defensive. Take feedback.

Tip #84

Always look at the rubric or assignment guidelines when you are revising.

The editing and revising process is also a good time to look over your assignment rubric and make sure you didn't leave out any key parts. For example, make sure you have the proper number of sources, you have written the right number of pages, or you meet your professor's other requirements. If you write a great paper but fail to meet some of the requirements on your assignment rubric, you won't score well. Forgetting aspects of the rubric is a silly reason to lose points— don't make that mistake.

The Difference Between Editing And Revising

The words editing and revising are sometimes used interchangeably, but they have slightly different meanings. Revising refers to bigger changes in your paper, such as restructuring your ideas or adding additional points. Editing refers to smaller changes, such as word choice, punctuation, and grammar. Since revising deals with bigger picture issues, while editing involves little, specific problems, you should revise your paper first, and then edit it.

When you are editing and revising your paper, the most important thing you can do is ask yourself the question, "Why?" As a writer, why did you choose to include a particular quote or statistic? Why did you choose to exclude other information? How did you determine the structure of your paper? Why did you pick a particular word or phrase? Are there ways you could have presented your information that might have been better? Answering these questions will help you think about the best ways to modify your paper, and help distinguish you from other students and researchers who might have written about the same topic.

Questions to ask while you are revising

When revising your paper, you should address two main issues: the structure and content. Content refers to the ideas in your paper. Remember, the purpose of the paper is to support your thesis. Ask yourself if the ideas in your paper link back to your thesis? Ideas that don't relate to your thesis can distract your reader and obscure the key points that you want to make. While they may be interesting, your paper is probably stronger without them.

Do you have enough content?

To make sure you have properly supported your thesis, look back at your thesis statement and break it down into its main points. Once you have a list of these main points, read back through your paper and identify evidence that supports each point. Each main point in your paper should be justified by several pieces of evidence.

If after reading your paper you realize that you have left some of your main points unsupported, you have two options. You must either rework your thesis statement so it fits the evidence in your paper, or you must add more evidence to the body of your paper to back up your thesis. Either of these methods can work. Use your best judgment to decide which is more appropriate for your paper.

Content extends beyond just the basic facts that support your thesis statement. You must also make sure that your paper presents enough information and context to make your evidence understandable to your reader. Are there places where your reader might be confused? Is there additional information from your research you need to include? For example, a scientific table full of data might be important evidence which supports your thesis. However, if you don't explain what the data in the table means, your reader may be bewildered by all the numbers. Make sure you provide enough background information so that your reader can understand the evidence in your paper.

Order and structure

Structure refers to the ordering of ideas in your paper. It is a good idea to look at your topic sentences — are they clear and specific? Do your body paragraphs contain evidence to back up your topic sentences? If your body paragraphs don't contain strong evidence then you aren't adequately supporting your thesis. If your body paragraphs contain strong evidence, but this evidence doesn't line up with the topic sentences, consider rewriting your topic sentences or reworking the structure of your paper.

You should also think about the order of your body paragraphs: Why did you choose that order? Now that you have written your paper, does that order make sense? Would a different order be better? Your argument will be much more persuasive if each paragraph follows logically from the previous one.

Transitions are also a key part of structure in your paper, and something you should consider as you are revising. Make sure your ideas flow together smoothly, and that you aren't hopping too abruptly from one paragraph to the next. If you've forgotten how transitions work, or need examples, look back at Chapter 6.

Basic Editing Tips

If you have finished revising your paper and are happy with its content and structure, you can begin editing. When you are editing, you aren't worried about your paper's thesis. Instead, you should be thinking about whether your words and sentences clearly convey your ideas.

Beyond spell-check

Many students think that editing is just about checking spelling and grammar. With computers and spell-check these days, editing almost seems unnecessary. But this is untrue. Although spell-check makes certain errors easy to spot, it does not catch everything. If you rely exclusively on spell-check for your editing, your paper will be left with some errors. For example, if you try to type the word "gear" but accidentally hit the "F" key, which is next to the "G" key on a standard keyboard, you will spell "fear." Depending on the context, spelling and grammar checks will likely ignore this mistake.

Typos and other mistakes like this happen often, so be sure to watch out for them while you are editing. When readers uncover grammar and editing errors, they tend to believe the research is lower quality and that the writer does not care about their work. You have worked really hard on your research paper — don't let people discredit you because of spelling mistakes.

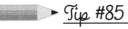 *Tip #85*

Don't trust your word processing program to edit your work for you. Editing is about more than just spelling and grammar.

In addition to checking for spelling and grammar, editing means ensuring that your sentences are clear and your word choices are accurate. For example, Chapter 6 discussed how to avoid passive voice in your writing. When you are editing, you should look for sentences that are in passive voice, and switch them to active voice. Remember, active voice tends to flow better and makes your writing more vibrant.

How to catch your mistakes

You are probably used to looking at your paper on the computer. After all, you spent many hours typing it. These days, many professors even have students submit their papers electronically, meaning you never have to print your paper at all.

 *Tip #86*

If possible, print your paper and edit it by hand.

However, printing your paper can make the editing process much more worthwhile. Editing your paper by hand will allow you to look at it with a fresh set of eyes and forces you to think more deeply about changes. You might notice something wrong with your paper when you are reading the print copy, and write down a way to correct it. When you go to fix your paper on your computer, you'll have to think about the correction again, which will help you come up with the best possible change.

 *Tip #87*

Read your paper aloud when you are editing.

Reading out loud requires a higher level of concentration compared to reading silently. You will remain more focused on the words that are actually on the page, which will allow you to spot errors more easily. You are also more likely to notice passages that sound clunky or poorly worded. If you stumble reading a section, consider changing it so it rolls off the tongue more cleanly.

If you feel weird reading your paper aloud, you can use a computer software to read your paper to you instead.

Tip #88

Copy your entire paper and paste it into an online translator that has an audio feature. Don't worry about another language — tell the translator to go from English to English, and then play the audio. Listen closely, and you'll hear any grammar mistakes or typos.

While following these techniques will help you edit your paper, editing is often easier if you know what sort of mistakes to look for. Many professors will tell you that students commonly make the same errors in their writing. The next chapter will address these common mistakes and give advice to help you avoid them.

Chapter 9
Common Writing Mistakes

As this book has mentioned many times, you are not the first student to write a research paper in college. This means that the mistakes you will likely make when writing your paper are mistakes that many other students have made before. This chapter will outline these common writing mistakes and tell you how to fix them, so the final version of your paper can be error-free.

Things To Watch Out For

One mistake many students make is overusing their favorite words. Maybe you like the transition word "however." Maybe you describe everything as "essential," or introduce every piece of evidence with the phrase "for example." Your reader will notice if you use the same words or phrases over again and may become more focused on that word or phrase than your argument.

 *Tip #89*

> Use the search function to see what words you might be using too often, and then look up some synonyms.

For example, let's say you overuse the word "often" in your writing. According to the thesaurus, some synonyms are: generally, usually, frequently, regularly, normally, typically, and repeatedly. Depending on the context, you can probably substitute these words and make your writing less repetitive.

Homophones

The English language is full of homophones — words that have the same pronunciation but different spellings. You are probably familiar with many homophones, "see" and "sea," "plane" and "plain," and "read" and "red," for example. While these homophones are all fairly simple to understand, some homophones are more subtle and are used less frequently. As a result, students are more likely to make mistakes. The following table contains examples of homophones that students commonly misunderstand. Keep in mind, this list is incomplete. If you are wondering about other homophones, look up a list online.

 *Tip #90*

Watch out for homophones: words that sound the same, but are spelled differently. Spellcheck won't typically catch these mistakes.

Commonly Mistaken Homophones	Correct Usage
Your and You're	"Your" is a possessive word indicating ownership. (Ex: Do not forget your movie tickets). "You're" is a contraction of the words "you" and "are." (Ex: Are you sure you're going to come with us to the movie?)
Its and It's	"Its" with no apostrophe is the possessive form of the pronoun "it." (Ex: The dog wagged its tail). "It's" is a contraction of the words "it" and "is." (Ex: It's a big dog).
There, Their, and They're	"There" is used to indicate a place. (Ex: Do not park there). "Their" is the possessive of the pronoun "they." (Ex: We got here in their car). "They're" is a contraction of the words "they" and "are." (Ex: They're bringing the car).
Accept and Except	"Accept" is a verb, which typically means to receive something. (Ex: I accept my mom's suggestion). "Except" is a preposition, which indicates excluding something. (Ex: I accepted all of her suggestions, except the one about my thesis statement).
All right and Alright	"Alright" is a shortening of the phrase "All right." In your formal writing, you should always use "All right." (Ex: It is not all right to use "alright" in your writing).

Commonly Mistaken Homophones	Correct Usage
All together and Altogether	"All together" means collectively, or at the same time. (Ex: We edited our papers all together during class). "Altogether" means entirely. (Ex: I am altogether too tired to keep editing my paper).
Who's and Whose	"Who's" is a contraction of "who is." (Ex: Who's the author of this great paper?) "Whose" is a possessive pronoun. (Ex: Whose thesis statement is this?)
Assure, Ensure, and Insure	"Assure" is to convince someone of something, usually in a positive way. (Ex: His mother assured him that everything would be all right). "Ensure" is to secure or make sure. (Ex: His mother ensured he had something to eat by bringing his lunch to school). "Insure" is to guarantee against loss. (Ex: His mother insured his car, because she figured he would probably crash it).
Then and Than	"Then" is typically used as an adverb to reference a time. (Ex: Back then, movie tickets only cost five cents). "Than" is a conjunction, used to compare two or more things. (Ex: Movie tickets are more expensive than they used to be).
Affect and Effect	"Affect" is a verb that means to impact or produce change on something. (Ex: The documentary deeply affected him.) "Effect" is a noun that means an impact, result, or consequence. (Ex: Although the documentary was deeply moving, it had no political effect.)

Like other grammatical and spelling mistakes, misusing homophones hurts your credibility as a writer, and your professor will almost certainly take off points for it. If you know a word is a homophone, or if you are unsure exactly which word to use, look it up! It's always better to spend a few extra minutes with the dictionary than to have a silly mistake in your paper.

The punctuation situation

Punctuation can be surprisingly difficult for college students. Punctuation isn't just a matter of grammar — although you will certainly look foolish if you mess that up. It also affects the flow and rhythm of your paper. Knowing how to properly use various punctuation marks will make your writing seem smooth and professional, while misusing punctuation will likely annoy your professor and cost you points.

Uses and misuses of the semicolon

 *Tip #91*

Be very careful with your use of the semi-colon.

The semi-colon is a peculiar punctuation mark. Many students try to use them in place of commas or to connect items on a list. Semi-colons should be used in exactly two cases: when separating items in a list that already involve commas and as a connection between two complete thoughts. Take a look at the following few examples, which show incorrect and correct semi-colon use:

Incorrect example: There were three finalists in the talent show: the girls who sang Johnny Horton's "The Battle of New Orleans"; the boy who rode his unicycle; and the group that danced to the song "1985."

Corrected example: There were three finalists in the talent show: the girls who sang Johnny Horton's "The Battle of New Orleans," the boy who rode his unicycle, and the group that danced to the song "1985."

Incorrect example: The committee narrowed down their search for a new headquarters to the following cities: Poughkeepsie, New York, Denver, Colorado, Kalispell, Montana, and Los Angeles, California.

Correct example: The committee narrowed down their search for a new headquarters to the following cities: Poughkeepsie, New York; Denver, Colorado; Kalispell, Montana; and Los Angeles, California.

In the first example about the talent show, the items in the list do not include commas themselves, so commas should be used to separate them. However, semi-colons are necessary in the second example. Otherwise, it would be unclear for the reader whether "New York" referenced a city or a state. In this case, the semi-colon serves as a super-comma.

If you are using a semi-colon to connect two complete thoughts, you must be able to substitute a period in its place. Why would you use a semi-colon instead of a period? A semi-colon indicates a connection between ideas or thoughts in a way a period might not.

Incorrect example: John needs new glasses, he can barely read the newspaper in the mornings.

Correct example: John needs new glasses. He can barely read the newspaper in the mornings.

Correct example: John needs new glasses; he can barely read the newspaper in the mornings.

In this case, both the second and third examples are grammatically correct. The semi-colon connects the two clauses more than the period does, and thus changes the rhythm slightly. Read the examples aloud and see if you can notice a different.

Now that you know how to use semi-colons properly, you might want to use them all the time. Resist the urge — semi-colons are best used sparingly. By connecting sentences that could otherwise be separate, semi-colons speed up the pace of your writing. In certain cases, you may want to do this. However, if you use the semi-colon too frequently, your writing will seem too fast-paced, and your reader might feel rushed.

Sentence errors

Run-on sentences, comma splices, and fragments are three errors that many students make, all of which have to do with improperly-written sentences. Run-on sentences occur when two independent clauses are connected incorrectly. Two independent clauses must always be connected with a period, a semi-colon, or a conjunction. (If you need a review on clauses or conjunctions, look back at Chapter 6).

 *Tip #92*
_____

Watch out for fragments, run-on sentences, and comma splices.

If the two independent clauses are connected by a comma, the run-on sentence is known as a comma splice. Comma splices are fairly easy to spot because the clause before the comma and the clause after the comma will both work as stand-alone sentences. You can correct this error by adding a conjunction, changing the comma to a period and creating two separate sentences, or using a semi-colon. Take a look at the following examples.

Run-on sentence example: The general ordered the strike he thought it would help win the war.

Comma splice example: The general ordered the strike, he thought it would help win the war.

Correct example #1: The general ordered the strike; he thought it would help win the war.

Correct example #2: The general ordered the strike. He thought it would help win the war.

Correct example #3: The general ordered the strike because he thought it would help win the war.

Both the run-on sentence and the comma splice example are grammatically incorrect. The corrected examples show different ways the sentence could be written; each has a slightly different effect. Read through the correct examples again, and see if you can notice a difference in the pacing of the sentences.

Fragments are the opposite of run-on sentences. A fragment is a phrase that is intended to be sentence but lacks a subject, a verb, and a complete thought. Some writers think that fragments can add emphasis, but in a formal research paper, you should avoid them. Because fragments occur when the writer leaves out the subject, verb, or complete thought, resolving a fragment typically requires adding something to your sentence. You can also resolve a fragment by incorporating it with the surrounding sentences. Take a look at the following examples.

Fragment example: The chains rattling as they fall.

Corrected example: The chains were rattling as they fell.

Fragment example: Running through the forest, leaping over fallen trees.

Corrected example: The boy ran through the forest, leaping over fallen trees.

Fragment example: The general was planning on ordering the strike eventually. Perhaps after the rainstorm.

Corrected example: The general was planning on ordering the strike, perhaps after the rainstorm.

Hyphens and dashes

Hyphens and dashes are two other fickle punctuation marks that you should make sure to study. The hyphen and the en dash connect words, while the em dash separates phrases or clauses. Both types of dashes are longer than hyphens, and em dashes typically have a space on either side, while en dashes and hyphens do not.

Tip #93

Know the difference between dashes and hyphens, and use both properly.

You always use hyphens when you are using compound adjectives — groups of two or more adjectives that come before a noun. Compound adjectives are hyphenated; however, a series of adjectives are not hyphenated when they come after a noun. Take a look at the following examples, which show when to use (and not to use) a hyphen.

My two-year-old cousin made me a birthday card.

My cousin turned two years old last week.

I love this well-lit room!

The room was well lit.

Some words you know use hyphens all the time, such as "year-old" and "back-to-back." Any word that starts with "self" is always hyphenated, such as "self-care" or "self-esteem." You also always use hyphens before a number, such as "post-2000." If you are unsure about whether to hyphenate, look it up online or ask a professor or tutor.

The en dash, like the hyphen, is used to connect words, specifically words that represent a span of numbers or time. The en dash is slightly longer than the hyphen, but is shorter than the em dash. The following examples show how to use the en dash.

The 2010–2011 season was the team's best.

The professor holds office hours every Wednesday, 8:00–9:30.

By a vote of 9–4, the town council passed the measure.

The story appeared in the January–March issue of the magazine.

However, you should not use the en dash if your range follows the prepositions "from" or between." In these cases, you should write out the sentence, as shown in the following examples

The professor holds office hours every Wednesday from 8:00 to 9:30.

President McKinley held the office between 1897 and 1901.

The rules for using em dashes are a bit more flexible than the rules for hyphens and en dashes. When used sparingly, em dashes can add emphasis and make your writing more effective. Generally, em dashes are used to accentuate a particular phrase or clause. You can use a set of dashes in the middle of a sentence or a single dash to set off material at the beginning or end of a sentence. Take a look at the following examples.

Example without em dashes: Many variables in both the United States and Latin America influence immigration.

Example with em dashes: Many variables — in both the United States and Latin America — influence immigration.

Both of these examples are grammatically correct. The second example uses em dashes to set off the prepositional phrase "in both the United States and Latin America." The em dashes add more emphasis to this phrase and make it stand out. A writer would choose to use em dashes in this case if this phrase was especially important.

Em dashes can also replace other punctuation marks, such as periods. The em dash typically makes the sentence or sentences stand out, as shown in the following examples.

Example without em dashes: The general didn't order the strike. He thought the enemy wouldn't attack.

Example with em dashes: The general didn't order the strike — he thought the enemy wouldn't attack.

Once again, both of these examples are grammatically correct. The example that uses em dashes creates more emphasis than the sentence that only uses periods. Em dashes can also be used to insert a clause into the middle of a sentence, as shown in the next example.

Example: As the company has grown — it now has five times as many factories as it did in 1990 — its environmental impact has also skyrocketed.

In this example, the clause "it now has five times as many factories as it did in 1990" provides additional information that is helpful to the sentence. Em dashes are grammatically necessary in this case in order to set off the clause from the remainder of the sentence.

Em dashes are a helpful punctuation mark and can make your writing more effective. However, you should be careful not to overuse them. If you use dashes too often they will become less meaningful and your writing may seem jumpy. As a general rule, don't use more than one set of em dashes in a paragraph.

While the hyphen is available on the keyboard—it is located next to the "0" key—there is no key on a typical keyboard to insert either type of dash. Most word processing softwares allow you to insert a dash by going to the "insert" tab, and clicking on "symbol" or "special character," depending on which software you are using. If you can't figure out how to insert a dash on your own, you can always search "em dash" or "en dash" on the internet and then copy and paste.

Other writing notes

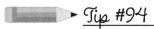 *Tip #94*

Avoid using an unattached "this."

Improper use of the word "this" is another common writing mistake. When you are writing formally, you want to use the word "this" exclusively as an adjective, not a noun. When the word "this" is not followed by a noun, it can be difficult for your reader to tell what the word is referring to — a problem known as the unattached "this." Take a look at the following examples:

Incorrect example: This is a very pretty table.

Correct example: This table is very pretty.

Incorrect example: This shows how the global temperatures have actually increased substantially since the 1950s.

Correct example: This data show how the global temperatures have actually increased substantially since the 1950s.

 *Tip #95*

Don't confuse "less" and "fewer."

Writers commonly confuse the words "less" and "fewer." Both of these words generally reference a smaller quantity, but there is a key distinction. Use "fewer" when the quantity you are describing is countable or if the noun you are describing has a plural; use "less" when you would not be able to count the quantity or if the noun you are describing does not have a plural. Take a look at the following examples.

> There are fewer students in the class this year compared to last.
>
> The fish tank had less water after George spilled some.
>
> The Americans experienced fewer casualties during World War II than the Russians.
>
> The new president spends less time in the White House than his predecessor.

The number of students in a class and the number of Russian and American casualties during World War II can be counted, so "fewer" is the appropriate adjective. The nouns "water" and "time" do not have plural versions, so you should use "less" in these cases.

The Power of Less

Philosopher and mathematician Blaise Pascal once wrote: "I would have written a shorter letter, but I did not have the time."[9] Although Pascal lived in France during the 1600s, his observation is relevant to many students'

9. Tania Lombrozo, "This Could Have Been Shorter," *National Public Radio*. 3 Feb. 2014. Web.

writing today. Good writing is usually short and concise. When you are editing and revising your paper, ask yourself: "Could I say the same thing in fewer words?"

The word count issue

Imagine that you have almost finished your paper. You just need a few more lines — maybe your professor assigned a 12-page paper, but you've only written 11 pages. It's really tempting to repeat yourself a few times. You could restate your thesis three different ways in your conclusion. Or you could add a few meaningless sentences to one of your paragraphs. Don't do these things. Every sentence, even every word, in your paper should be there for a reason, and that reason shouldn't be "I needed to add some stuff to meet the requirements." If you add material that is off-topic, it will distract your reader. If it is repetitive, your reader will get bored.

 ▶ *Tip #96*

Many research paper assignments have word counts. Students often make the mistake of repeating themselves to try to reach a word count. If you finish writing your paper and realize that you are still short of the word count, go back and do more research. Don't repeat your same points in different words.

Writing concisely

So how do you make sure that every word in your paper means something? There is no single tip or trick that will make your writing smooth and concise, but there are a few guidelines you can follow.

Often, you can make your paper more concise by avoiding the use of adverbs. Adverbs are used to modify verbs, adjectives, or other adverbs. Many adverbs end in –ly. When you find yourself using adverbs in your writing, ask yourself if you could use a stronger verb or adjective instead. Consider the following example.

Wordy example: Global carbon emissions <u>increased very rapidly</u> following the Industrial Revolution.

This sentence has two adverbs. The word "rapidly" is an adverb modifying the verb, "increased." The word "very" is an adverb too, modifying the adverb "rapidly." Both of the adverbs serve to strengthen the extent of the verb, "increase." In this case, the sentence could be made stronger and more concise by removing these adverbs and using a strong verb, as shown in the next example.

Revised example: Global carbon emissions <u>skyrocketed</u> following the Industrial Revolution.

In this example, the strong verb "skyrocketed" eliminates the need for the adverbs. It makes the sentence more concise and powerful. If you are looking to reduce adverbs and use stronger verbs in your writing, you might find it helpful to look up verbs in a thesaurus.

As the examples with adverbs show, using strong, clear words is better than using many words. The next few examples show other ways you can make your writing more concise by replacing a string of weak words with a few strong ones.

> *Wordy example*: President Lincoln <u>talked about the importance of</u> creating a nation based on freedom and equality for all.
>
> *Revised example*: President Lincoln <u>argued for</u> creating a nation based on freedom and equality for all.

> *Wordy example*: As a young man, Smith's work in the office of a famous New York lawyer <u>really helped make him believe that he wanted to change the world</u>.
>
> *Revised example*: As a young man, Smith's work in the office of a famous New York lawyer <u>instilled his desire to change the world</u>.

You can also make your writing less wordy by relying more on nouns, and less on verb phrases, as shown in the next example.

> *Wordy example*: The author's use of dark imagery demonstrates <u>how the protagonist has become severely depressed because of the trauma he has experienced</u>.
>
> *Revised example*: The author's use of darkness imagery demonstrates <u>the protagonist's depression resulting from his trauma</u>.

These examples show just a few of the ways you can make your writing more concise. Ultimately, writing style varies from person to person, and there is no single rulebook for how to make your writing sound sleek and impressive. As long as you make concise writing a goal, you will be on the path to success.

Chapter 10
The Finishing Touches

If you've written and edited your paper in advance of the deadline, you are well on a path toward success. This chapter will address the finishing touches—the small details about your paper that you want to make right before you turn in your paper.

The modifications addressed in this chapter will only have a small impact on your paper's score. If you write a mediocre paper, you can't save it with a great title. If you don't cite your sources properly, it won't matter that you used the proper font size for your footnotes.

Nonetheless, you want to make sure to put these finishing touches on your paper before you turn in your final draft. Some professors will take off points if your formatting is incorrect. Others may not officially score formatting, but will certainly be annoyed if you pick a hard-to-read font or wrongly-sized margins. You've come this far with your research and writing—it's worthwhile to take a few extra minutes to ensure you turn in the most polished product.

The Title

The title of your paper will be the first thing your reader sees, but it is hardly the most important part. While there's no specific rulebook when it comes to writing titles, the goal of your title is to engage the reader with your work. Some professors like to see clever, funny titles. Others would rather that your title be straightforward and to-the-point.

> A clever or funny title might engage your reader and draw them in, like a good hook in your introduction. However, some students try too hard to be funny and come up with a title that is irrelevant to their topic or argument. If humor doesn't come naturally to you, don't waste your time trying to make your title funny.

Your title should always be relevant to your topic and give your reader a basic understanding of what your paper is about. Your title should not be long—it shouldn't take more than a line on your computer screen. The following examples are hypothetical titles for some of the paper topics that have been discussed in this book.

Fossil Fuels and Global Temperatures

Preschool Policy: The Implications of Early Childhood Development Research

Not a Superman: Guilt and Philosophy in Fyodor Dostoevsky's *Crime and Punishment*

As you'll notice with each of these titles, you should always capitalize the first word of your title, as well as any word that comes after a colon. You should also capitalize all other important words—only prepositions (such as of, from, and in) and articles (a, an, and the) should be lowercase. If your paper is analyzing a particular document or source, you should give the name of the source and its author in your title.

Tip #97

The title might be the first thing your reader sees, but it's not actually the most important part of your paper. It's nice to have a clever title, but don't waste your time agonizing over it—the rest of your paper is more important!

Formatting Your Paper

Most of this book has discussed the actual content of your paper—the words that explain your argument. The formatting of your paper refers to its appearance, which is based on factors like font, size, spacing, alignment, margins, headers, and footers. The citation styles discussed in Chapter 5 (MLA, Turabian, and APA) also come with formatting recommendations, which you can look up. Your professor may also have specific formatting requirements. Make sure to look at your rubric or ask!

Why formatting matters

If you've already spent many hours writing and researching, taking the time to standardize your fonts and insert page numbers might seem annoying. By this point, you probably really want to be done with your paper. However, many professors will grade your formatting.

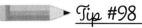 *Tip #98*

> Formatting might seemed silly, but it does affect how readable your paper is. Make sure you use a professional font, such as Arial or Times New Roman. Make sure that the font and the text size are the same throughout the paper.

Some professors have very specific formatting requirements. They may mention on the rubric their preferred font, text size, margin size, or other factors. Make sure you check for these requirements — if you don't, you may lose points, or put your professor in a bad mood when they are reading your paper.

How to format

The software you use to write your paper (such as Microsoft Word or Google Docs) likely has all the tools you need to edit your paper. Use the toolbar at the top of the document. If you're not sure about a specific formatting issue, you can always perform an internet search; typing in "How to insert page numbers in Microsoft Word," into a search engine will yield some helpful results, because you're not the first person to wonder.

➤ *Tip #99*

Many professors ask students to include headers, footers, or page numbers.

Keep in mind that you might run into formatting issues if you transfer between file types (such as converting from Microsoft Word to Google Docs or vice versa). You should double-check your file extensions to make sure you are saving in a format that can be read by multiple programs, such as .doc.

Typically, your research paper should be double-spaced. You should use one-inch margins, unless you professor specifies otherwise. Your font should be either Times New Roman or Arial. You should use size 12 font for your entire paper, although you may use a smaller size for footnotes or endnotes. You should indent every paragraph, but avoid extra line spaces between paragraphs. You should include page numbers, either in the header (the top margin) or the footer (the bottom margin) — your professor might tell you which one.

Some professors also ask you to include your last name in the header or footer, alongside the page number. If you modify the header or footer of your document, those changes will appear in the header or footer on every page, so make sure you are careful about the changes you make.

The specific steps you follow to format your paper can vary between computers and file types. If you can't figure out a specific issue, ask a friend, a tutor, a professor or a librarian. This also means you shouldn't completely leave formatting for the last minute — you don't want to be scrambling to figure out headers or page numbers the night before your paper is due.

When you are formatting your paper, you should also double-check your works cited or bibliography. Most citation styles require specific formats — and you really don't want to mess up citing your sources.

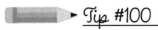 *Tip #100*

Pictures and other visuals can often mess with the formatting of your paper. Make sure to look over your paper after you print it to make sure everything is in the right place before you hand it in.

Turning in your paper

Many professors still ask students to turn in a print copy of their paper. However, these days, it is increasingly common for students to submit papers electronically. If you are turning in a hard copy of your paper, do one last check of the formatting after you have printed it.

If you are turning in your paper electronically, make sure to check which file format your professor prefers. Some professors may prefer a PDF document, while others may ask you to submit a Word document, or even use a software like Google Docs. Some professors may not care, but if yours does, you want to make sure you turn in your paper correctly.

Afterwards

Many students think they are done once they submit the final version of their paper. They pat themselves on the back, and put the whole topic out of their minds, feeling grateful that they never have to think about it again.

Actually, you shouldn't give up all memories of your paper the second you are finished. You will have to write research papers again in the future. It's OK to give yourself a break once you've finished your paper, but it's important to take away some lessons too.

Don't stop learning

Turning in a paper that you are proud of is a very satisfying feeling. Finding out a few weeks later that you scored well also feels really good. But even if you've written a great paper and received a grade you are happy with, you still have room for improvement.

➤ Tip #101

> When you are finished with your paper, you might want to never think about it again. However, you will probably have to write similar papers in the future. Make sure to read the feedback you receive from your professor so you can figure out how to do better in the future.

A good professor will give you feedback on your research paper, even if you receive a good grade. Make sure to reread your paper and your professor's comments. Take note, and think about what you can do better on your next paper.

In addition to the feedback you receive from your instructor, you should take some time to reflect on what you learned from the research paper process. You hopefully learned a lot about your research topic. You acquired skills, like using databases, writing thesis statements, and editing your own work, and you may also have learned something about yourself as a writer and researcher.

Writing research papers is about the process as much as the final product. Ask yourself, which parts of the paper were most difficult for you? If you struggled with research, you might consider whether you picked too narrow of a topic, or whether you should look for sources in other places in the future. If you had trouble writing an introduction, you should remember to allow extra time for it the next time you write a paper. Maybe you learned that you are most productive at a certain time of day. Maybe you discovered that you're not the best with deadlines. Maybe you got really good advice from a friend. Remembering these facts about yourself will help with your papers in the future.

Congratulations on finishing your research paper, and best of luck with future ones!

Conclusion

Writing college-level research papers isn't easy. If it were, professors wouldn't make them a big deal, students wouldn't tell stories of late nights at the library, and there wouldn't be books like this one full of research and writing tips.

As with any skill, writing research papers won't suddenly become easy for you overnight. Writing takes practice, and everyone messes up along the way. Some students find that the writing process comes easily once they learn the basics. Others struggle with developing a style or constructing a strong, logical argument. Even students who are naturally talented make mistakes when they encounter a confusing topic or a new type of paper. Like learning an instrument or playing a sport, you will get better at writing a research paper every time you do it.

This book presented 101 tips to help you write your research paper and make your work stand out. Of these tips, I argue that Tip #6 is by far the most important. From Chapter 1:

Tip #6

While you are working on your research paper, try to find time to ask your professor questions if you encounter problems along the way. Many professors hold office hours or allow you to make an appointment to discuss your ideas. Some students think that asking many questions makes them seem stupid. In reality, it shows your professor or instructor that you care about succeeding.

No matter your skill level as a writer and researcher, knowing how to ask for help is perhaps the most important skill of all. Even if you are an experienced writer, you will someday encounter a paper topic that stumps you, or a professor who has different requirements than what you expect.

Many students who have written research papers in high school panic when they get to college and must cite their sources in Turabian instead of MLA. Others successfully write their first paper, only to freak out when they receive a grade that is not at the level they are used to. If you struggle—whether you are writing your first research paper or your tenth—it doesn't mean you should panic. It doesn't mean that writing isn't in your future, or that your class is too hard. It means that you are facing a task which you haven't faced before. Think back to the skills you have acquired, and ask about the issues that still stump you.

You might be wondering what the point of writing research papers is in the long-term—most adults don't write research papers for their day jobs. Unless you want to be a writer or an academic researcher, you might not have to write a full-length paper after you have finished college. But the skills you acquire from writing research papers carry over into nearly any field. Knowing how to craft an argument and persuade your reader will help you no matter what your career is. Writing and research skills—knowing how to determine which information is reliable and find answers to your questions—are likewise essential, especially with the unfortunate prevalence of misinformation on the internet. And even if you go into a career where all the skills you've learned from research papers seem irrelevant, learning to persevere when something is difficult will help you no matter what path you chose. So even if you know that writing research papers is not something you want to do in your future, the skills you will acquire will serve you well no matter where life takes you.

Author's Note

I wrote my first research paper when I was in seventh grade. It was about the Manhattan Project and the development of the first atomic bomb. I was a pretty enthusiastic middle-schooler, and I remember staying up late over Thanksgiving Break reading long academic books. By the time I wrote, revised, and turned in that paper, I thought it was basically the best paper in the world.

I don't go back and read that paper very often because it makes me cringe. (It is nowhere near the best paper in the world). Since then, I've written a lot of research papers, most of which have been much better. I've written a lot about history—topics ranging from apartheid in South Africa to American railroads in the 1870s—and about literature. One of my favorite papers I've ever written analyzed the choreopoem "For colored girls who have considered suicide / when the rainbow is enuf," by Ntozake Shange. I've written some papers for science classes, a few in economics, one in math, many in sociology, and a few entirely in Spanish, which is not my first language.

While all of the papers I have written are very different from one another, they still follow the same basic principles. They all had thesis statements and brought in evidence to support my argument. I have little doubt that writing each of them made me a stronger writer and student. The skills I learned researching novels and authors for an English literature class still applied when I was studying literature in Spanish. The ability to read primary sources that I gained when I was writing about the atomic bomb in seventh grade helped me write better history papers later on. The science papers I wrote in high school helped me analyze data for the economics papers I wrote in college, and the math paper I had to write taught me how to persevere through really tough assignments. In a lot of ways, writing research papers opened up a whole field of opportunities for me. For example, I never would have started writing books if I hadn't written many papers first.

Still, writing college-level research papers poses new challenges for any student. Even though I had written research papers before college, I found myself struggling to develop my own ideas, figure out different citation styles, and find strong sources about obscure topics. During my sophomore year of college, I spent an inordinate amount of time talking through ideas in my sociology professor's office hours, because I felt lost every time I looked at the prompts for his class. The sociology papers I wrote that semester weren't my best work, but I learned a lot from writing them.

Like any writer, I make plenty of mistakes. I've turned in papers with typos. I lost points for it; life went on. I've chosen paper topics only to realize they were incredibly boring; I've had to modify my thesis statement at the last minute when I encountered new evidence. I can tell you from personal experience that, no matter how easy a paper seems, trying to write it the night before is never, ever a good idea.

Despite some difficulties over the years, I can say with certainty that writing research papers does get easier. The more you read and learn and write, the more naturally these tasks will come. Don't be afraid to make mistakes. Don't be afraid to get insanely excited about a nerdy topic — someday, your ability to spew weird trivia facts will come in handy. Don't be afraid to work hard, and don't be afraid to ask for help when working hard isn't enough.

No matter your previous experiences or capabilities, writing a research paper shouldn't be a terribly painful experience. It should be something you learn from. So each time you finish a research paper, take a moment to be proud of what you've accomplished, and be ready to keep improving. That's all you can ask of yourself.

Glossary

Active voice: A sentence where the subject of the sentence completes the action described by the verb. For example: "The dog chased after the ball."

Alignment: the way text is set up on a page. For a research paper, you will want your text to be aligned left.

Anecdote: A short story describing a particular event.

Bias: The tendency of an author or source to promote a particular opinion or point of view.

Bibliography: A list of sources that were used for research, included at the end of a research paper.

Block quote: A quote of more than four lines, which is set on its own lines and indented.

Brainstorming: Generating ideas and drawing informal connections based on previous knowledge or research.

Cherry-picking: Selecting only certain facts (and omitting other ones) to make a certain point.

Clause: A phrase with a subject and a verb.

Comma splice: A grammatical error where two independent clauses are connected by a comma.

Complex sentence: A sentence containing one independent and one dependent clause.

Complex-compound sentence: A sentence containing two independent clauses connected by a coordinating conjunction and a dependent clause with a subordinating conjunction.

Compound sentence: A sentence containing two independent clauses connected by a coordinating conjunction.

Coordinating conjunction: A conjunction connecting two independents clauses. Coordinating conjunctions can be remembered with the acronym FANBOYS: for, and, no, but, or, yet and so.

Dash: A punctuation mark used to break up words or phrases.

Dependent clause: A clause beginning with a subordinating conjunction.

Editing: Making change changes to your paper, such as word choice and sentence structure.

Endnote: A form of inline citation that indicates the source for a particular quote, fact, or idea using a number in the text, which matches with a number included at the end of the paper.

Font: the standard appearance of type. For your research paper, you want to use a professional-looking font, such as Times New Roman.

Footer: the whitespace at the bottom of the page. For a research paper, you should allow at least one inch for a footer, although you may put a page number in that space.

Footnote: A form of inline citation that indicates the source for a particular quote, fact, or idea using a number in the text, which matches with a number included at the bottom of the page.

Fragment: A phrase intended a sentence that does not contain a full subject, verb, and complete thought.

Freewriting: A form of brainstorming where you write all your ideas about a particular topic or question, without worrying about spelling, grammar, order, or other considerations.

Header: the whitespace at the top of the page. For a research paper, you should allow at least one inch for a header, although you may put a page number in that space.

Homophone: A pair of words that sound alike but are spelled differently and have different meanings.

Hyphen: A punctuation mark used to bring together two words.

Independent clause: A phrase with a subject, verb, and complete thought which could stand alone as its own sentence.

Inline citations: Footnotes, endnotes, or parentheticals which indicate the source of a particular fact or idea in a research paper.

Inverted pyramid: A shape—which also resembles an upside-down triangle—which demonstrates the ideal structure for an introduction: starting out broad and narrowing.

Margin: the whitespace around the edges of the paper. For a research paper, you should typically use one-inch margins.

Mind-mapping: A brainstorming technique where you visually draw out connections between topics, using circles and lines.

Misquoting: Incorrectly quoting a source—you should never do this in your paper!

Outlining: Drafting a condensed, bullet-point version of your paper that shows the main ideas and the order they go in.

Paraphrase: Rewriting someone else's ideas in your own words.

Parenthetical citation: A form of inline citation that indicates the source for a particular quote, fact, or idea using parentheses (usually with the author's name and a page number) in the text.

Passive voice: A sentence where verb acts upon the subject of the sentence, and the person or thing that completes the action is omitted or described via a preposition phrase. For example: "The ball was chased after by the dog."

Peer-reviewed journal articles: Academic papers that—in addition to being written by a strong researcher— have been examined by other experts in the field to ensure accuracy.

Plagiarism: A form of cheating based on using someone else's words or ideas without giving them credit.

Primary source: A firsthand account of information without any analysis or interpretation.

Revising: Reading your paper after you have a complete draft and making necessary changes to its content and structure.

Rhetorical question: A question asked without an expected answer. Questions in research papers are almost always rhetorical—while the writer may be hoping to force the reader to think, the reader does not actually answer the question.

Run-on sentence: A grammatically incorrect sentence that occurs when two independent clauses are connected improperly.

Secondary source: A source written by researchers based on primary sources, and other secondary sources.

Simple sentence: A sentence made up of a single clause.

Size: with reference to fonts, the height and width of characters. For your research paper, you should typically use 12-point font.

Spacing: with reference to research papers, the amount of whitespace between lines. You should typically double-space your research paper.

Subordinating conjunction: A word that introduces a dependent clause. For example: after, although, because and since.

Summarize: Explaining someone else's ideas in a shorter, condensed version.

Tertiary sources: Encyclopedias, dictionaries, atlases, or other reference books used for background research.

Thesis: the central idea of a research paper.

Thesis statement: A sentence or two in the introduction which states the main argument of your paper.

Works cited: A list of sources that contributed specific facts or information, included at the end of a research paper.

Bibliography

"Americans with Criminal Records." *The Sentencing Project.* 2015. Web. **http://www.sentencingproject.org/wp-content/uploads/2015/11 /Americans-with-Criminal-Records-Poverty-and-Opportunity -Profile.pdf**. Accessed 14 Jul. 2017.

Dostoevsky, Fyodor. *Crime and Punishment.* Translated by Richard Pevear and Larissa Volokhonsky. New York: Vintage Books, 1992.

Keeling, M. J., and C. A. Gilligan. "Bubonic Plague: A Metapopulation Model of a Zoonosis." *Proceedings: Biological Sciences* 267, no. 1458 (2000): 2219-230. **http://www.jstor.org/stable/2665900**. Accessed 12 Jul. 2017.

Keyes, Ralph. "Ask Not Where This Quote Came From." *Washington Post.* 4 Jun. 2006. Web. **http://www.washingtonpost.com/wp-dyn/content /article/2006/06/02/AR2006060201406.html**. Accessed 14 Jul. 2017.

Kristof, Nicholas. "Smart Guns Save Lives. So Where Are They?" *New York Times.* 17 Jan. 2015. Web. **http://www.nytimes.com/2015/01/18 /opinion/sunday/nicholas-kristof-smart-guns-save-lives-so-where -are-they.html.** Accessed 13 Jul. 2017.

Lombrozo, Tania. "This Could Have Been Shorter." *National Public Radio*. 3 Feb. 2014. **http://www.npr.org/sections/13.7/2014/02/03 /270680304/this-could-have-been-shorter.** Accessed 14 Jul. 2017.

Peisner-Feinberg, Ellen S., and Margaret R. Burchinal. "Relations Between Preschool Children's Child-Care Experiences and Concurrent Development: The Cost, Quality, and Outcomes Study." *Merrill-Palmer Quarterly* 43, no. 3 (1997): 451-77. **http://www.jstor.org.ezproxy .bowdoin.edu/stable/23093333.** Accessed 12 Jul. 2017.

"Plagiarism." *Merriam-Webster Dictionary*. No date. Web. **http://www .merriam-webster.com/dictionary/plagiarism.** Accessed 14 Jul. 2017.

Sullivan, Edward T. *The Ultimate Weapon: The Race to Develop the Atomic Bomb*. New York: Holiday House, 2007.

World Bank. 2016. *Poverty and Shared Prosperity 2016: Taking on Inequality*. Washington, DC: World Bank. Web. **https://openknowledge .worldbank.org/bitstream/handle/10986/25078/9781464809583 .pdf.** Accessed 14 Jul. 2017.

Index

A

Active voice 93, 94, 127, 165
Analysis 17, 55, 56, 61, 72, 168
Anecdotes 106, 108

B

Background 37, 43, 57, 58, 125, 169
Bias 35, 41-43, 46, 48, 165
Bibliography 7, 8, 64, 65, 70, 71, 76, 154, 165, 171
Block quote 55, 99, 165
Brainstorming 5, 30, 31, 33, 80, 85, 165, 167

C

Claim 21, 22, 26, 63, 71, 83
Comma splice 137, 138, 166
Complex sentences 90
Complex-compound sentences 91
Compound sentence 89, 90, 166
Context 27, 29, 45, 52-54, 57, 59, 98, 113, 122, 125, 127, 132

Coordinating conjunction 89, 90, 166

D

Dashes 39, 141, 142
Deadline 13, 18, 82, 149
Draft 18, 28, 31, 61, 82, 120, 121, 149, 168

E

Experiment 6, 18, 36, 37

F

Fact checking 41, 44
Font 14, 83, 149, 151-153, 166, 169
Footnotes 70, 74-76, 149, 153, 167
Fragment 138, 139, 167
Freewriting 30, 167

H

Header 153, 167
Homophones 8, 132, 133, 135

I

Inline citations 65, 68, 70, 71, 76, 100, 167
Inverted pyramid 105, 112, 114, 167

M

Mind-mapping 31, 167
Misinformation 39, 46, 159
Misquoting 6, 68, 168

O

Office hours 19, 140, 141, 158, 162
Outlining 31, 168

P

Paraphrase 65-67, 76, 168
Parenthetical citations 70, 74, 75
Passive voice 93, 94, 127, 168
Planning 5, 21, 57, 61, 85, 139
Primary sources 36, 38, 43, 45, 162, 169

R

Reference 37, 43, 87, 89, 134, 144, 169
Rhetorical question 92, 168
Rubric 19, 84, 123, 152
Run-on sentence 137, 138, 168

S

Secondary sources 37, 72, 169
Simple sentence 89, 90, 169

Subordinating conjunction 90, 91, 166, 169
Summarizing 6, 17, 55, 58, 65, 67

T

Tertiary sources 6, 37, 169

W

Works cited 65, 70, 71, 76, 154, 169